THE POSSIBILITY WHEEL

THE POSSIBILITY WHEEL

Making better choices in a fractured world

Patricia Lustig
and
Gill Ringland

Triarchy Press

Published in this First Edition in 2024 by:
Triarchy Press
Axminster, England

info@triarchypress.net
www.triarchypress.net

Copyright © Patricia Lustig and Gill Ringland 2024

The right of Patricia Lustig and Gill Ringland to be identified as the authors of this work has been asserted by them in accordance with the Copyright, Designs and Patents Act, 1988.

No part of this publication may be reproduced, stored in a retrieval system or transmitted in any form or by any means including photocopying, electronic, mechanical, recording or otherwise, without the prior written permission of the publisher.

All rights reserved.

A catalogue record for this book is available from the British Library.

Print ISBN: 978-1-917251-05-1
ePub ISBN: 978-1-917251-06-8

CONTENTS

Chapter 1	Introduction	1
PART ONE	Threats	7
Chapter 2	Introduction to Part One	9
Chapter 3	Fractured Backbones	15
Chapter 4	Global Heating	24
Chapter 5	Breakdown of International Relations	32
Chapter 6	Collapse of Global Health	40
PART TWO	Forces for Change	47
Chapter 7	Introduction to Part Two	49
Chapter 8	Population	53
Chapter 9	Urban Pull	60
Chapter 10	Mobility	66
Chapter 11	Energy Choices	73
Chapter 12	Connected World	80
Chapter 13	AI	87
Chapter 14	Biology	94
Chapter 15	Planetary Limits	100
Chapter 16	Economic Activity	107
Chapter 17	Social Change	117
Chapter 18	Pulling it all Together	127
PART THREE	The Possibility Wheel	131
Chapter 19	Introduction to Part Three	133
Chapter 20	The Possibility Wheel Tool	136
Chapter 21	Example: Fractured Backbones	143
Chapter 22	Example: Global Heating	148
Chapter 23	Example: Breakdown in International Relations	153
Chapter 24	Example: Collapse of Global Health	158
Chapter 25	Insights	163
Appendix 1	UN Sustainable Development Goals for 2030	170
Appendix 2	Terminology and some sources of data	172
	Index	174
	About the Authors	178
	About the Publisher	179

FIGURES

Fig 1	Sources of global greenhouse gas emissions	25
Fig 2	Earth is Heating Up	26
Fig 3	Global population forecasts	53
Fig 4	Life Expectancy	55
Fig 5	Japan and Nigeria 2040	56
Fig 6	Migration to urban areas	60
Fig 7	Passenger Vehicle numbers 1980-2035	68
Fig 8	CO_2 emitted per kWh generated	74
Fig 9	The Countries with the Highest Density of Robot Workers	89
Fig 10	Biodiversity risk hotspots	101
Fig 11	Water shortage 2025	103
Fig 12	Income distribution	108
Fig 13	Living conditions and inequality	110
Fig 14	The Doughnut of social and planetary boundaries	112
Fig 15	Seven Ways to think like a 21st-century economist	122

Acknowledgements

We have been encouraged and sustained by a large circle of family, friends, colleagues and reviewers as we developed the ideas in this book.

People who have sustained us: Nic Pulford for coffees, teas, and encouragement; Jenny Schultz for a kind ear, Beverley Kracher, Richard Hames, Jonathan Blanchard Smith, Chris Skelly, Wendy Schultz, Phil Davison. Special thanks to Sarah Jackson for her help with our title and to Michael Mainelli and Simon Mills for publishing some of our work based on the book as we developed it, in the Long Finance Pamphleteer blogs.

Special thanks to those who have agreed to be 'guinea pigs': Anne Kyoya, Ed Steinmuller, Samista Jugwand, Ashish Manwar, Kelly Evans, Joe Little, Aida Ponce Del Castillo, Mike Jackson, and Laura Schleuber.

This book has also benefitted from the insights of the Emerging Fellows of the Association of Professional Futurists, from across the globe. They are: Anne Kyoya, Chris Mayer, Seth Harrell, Ashish Manwar, Raquel Valenca, Asma Zainal, Steven Lichty, Heba Al-Hadyian, Samista Jugwand, Khai Seng Hong, Zabrina Epps, Cesar Perez, Grace Okubo, amalia deloney, Rachal Magaji, Wensupu Yang, Elena Krafft and Suneet Pansare.

And last but not least, we appreciate the staff at Triarchy Press and especially our editor, Andrew Carey, for his enthusiasm and understanding and for insisting that our writing be absolutely clear. He is the best editor we have worked with – and a real pleasure working together.

Chapter 1 – Introduction

Why we wrote this book

In many ways, the world is in a better state than ever before.

The last two centuries of economic growth mean that billions are no longer poor. People live longer and their lives are far healthier. It is now becoming clear that this phase of economic growth is coming to an end as we bump up against the physical limits of our planet[1].

At the Davos World Economic Forum in January 2023, Sven Smit, head of the McKinsey Global Institute told Gillian Tett, "We are on the cusp of a new era. But we don't really know what that is, or even what it should be called" [2].

So what is coming now? No one knows. The changes that mark the end of this historic phase of economic growth make it difficult to make decisions. And the quality of decisions made by organisations and governments affects us all: decisions made with old paradigm assumptions may not be able to take advantage of opportunities presented by the new, emerging paradigm.

At the same time, the world has coped with the disruptive effect of the Covid-19 pandemic, the economic damage of financial systems failure, the tragedy of conflicts, the impact of volatile energy prices and inflation. People are encountering disruptive changes and threats in a way that most have not experienced in their lifetimes. As we connected with our worldwide network, we observed that many people are struggling to make decisions in this time of extreme disruption.

This book provides a descriptive and analytic framework for making sense of the data on what is happening across the world. We base our evidence on the best sources we can find[3], which is important when so much news is skewed and oriented towards what sells: 'bad news'. Our framework uses the term 'Forces for Change' to describe the visible, paradigm changing, outcomes of economic growth over the past two centuries. It uses the term 'Threats' for the disruptive forces at work. One of the less discussed outcomes of the changing paradigm is that systems and rules are breaking down in the emerging political, societal and economic world order. Within the framework we introduce a new concept: Backbone. We use the phrase *Fractured Backbones* to explore the implications of this breakdown.

We have found that people facing the challenge of making decisions need more than an analytic framework for describing the outside world. They need a toolset to capture the implications of the global evidence, for their world and for the decisions they need to make. So we provide a toolset which uses the framework and helps people to investigate and create additional resilient choices. The toolset brings the global evidence to play in your locality and organisational context, to develop a range of choices. With choices to stimulate ideas, you can explore more opportunities, make more robust decisions, enjoy better outcomes.

That is why we wrote this book.

In the next section we discuss some of the hurdles to finding and understanding the evidence from data about the world. We describe the framework in more detail, before describing the tool – the Possibility Wheel – which helps you develop resilient choices and make more robust decisions. Finally we provide a practical section called 'Using this book'.

Evidence, optimism and pessimism

So, what is really happening in the external world?

One hurdle to seeing what is really happening is that so much of the commentary on world news, events and trends is full of fear. It is not just the daily and weekly media, where we know that bad news sells. For instance, books on climate change range from science fiction[4] to scholarly reports[5]. They mostly anticipate doom.

We, however, are pragmatic optimists. As one of our blogs[6] explains, "The first, second and third reason [for optimism] is that the serious financial media are saying that electricity generated from renewables is now [written in December 2022] cheaper than that from fossil fuels[7]. The implications of this change are immense. The essential infrastructure change will of course be a limiting factor, but money often talks. According to Fatih Birol, executive director of IEA, solar and wind are replacing much of the gas withheld by Russia, "with the uptick in coal appearing to be relatively small and temporary". For the first time, in 2023, the IEA said global fossil fuel use could peak by 2030 thanks to stronger global emissions policies[8]. We would add "…and relative price changes".

On a wider front, a recent book by Hannah Ritchie[9] brings together evidence based on data collected through the Our World in Data[10] publication. Its title is *Not the End of the World: How we can be the first generation to build a sustainable planet*, which is self-explanatory!

Throughout this book, we refer to the power of ideas and technology to change the question and find new paradigms.

From this evidence and other sources, we recognise that there are *reasons* for optimism. But at the same time we are realistic about the Threats facing the world. As we write, geopolitical tensions are rising and they are alarming in a way not seen in recent decades.

We believe that times of great change can also be times of great possibility and opportunity. We have seen that challenges create opportunity as well as risk. We have observed that pragmatic optimists are the ones with the ideas for progress, the energy to take these ideas forward, the self-confidence to try and the willingness to learn if it does not work the first time. If you have the courage to be pragmatically optimistic and believe that you can make a difference, this book will help you to see how you can do so.

We aim to show you that the future need not actually be overwhelming… nor scary: we provide tools to increase your agency and your *sense* of agency. By considering the causes of change we provide a more holistic view of the world in which we live, and hence see the beginnings of potential future developments.

Throughout the book, we focus on people. We share Rutger Bregman's view that it is realistic to assume that people are good; and we recommend his book,[11] *Humankind*.

The past few years have provided unexpected lessons on how business and society cope with shocks and uncertainty. As Ikea executive Jasper Brodin says[12], "Look at what people have gone through: the pandemic, the economic damage, the tragedy of war, energy prices. What people might have underestimated is human resilience."

This book is for those who have the energy and passion to make the world fit for people today – as well as for their children and grandchildren in the future.

How this book helps you create more resilient choices to support robust decisions

The starting point for this book is the recognition that we live in uncertain and alarming times. The evidence on what is really happening is often messy and can be contradictory. To help bring some clarity, we have found it useful when describing a messy world to distinguish two qualitatively different sources of change.

The first source of change is Threats. Threats are actually already happening, and the impacts are sudden and big. For instance, *Global Heating* is already causing disruptive, extreme weather across the world. But you can also draw on Threats that are happening to consider what further events and effects might emerge. This will help you to think about what you might do about them.

Our biggest 'ah-ha' came as we developed our analysis of the Threats. The three that we chose had measurable outcomes. However, we soon realised that there was something connecting them – threads that join up and influence the outcomes from these three Threats. We called these connectors 'Backbones'.

Backbones are agreed upon sets of rules which support the way that things work. They are based upon the rule of law and shared assumptions. Backbones cover many aspects of life such as financial services, governance, and international (technical and professional) standards. We noticed that the impact of the three initial Threats would be more or less dependent on – and reduced by – the existence of functioning Backbones. Then we observed that a number of Backbones which have been important over the past decades are no longer fit for purpose: fractured or fracturing, rather than evolving.

We felt that *Fractured Backbones* was, therefore, the most significant Threat, as it refers to the structures that can mitigate or support adaptation to the other three, widely discussed, Threats. So we investigated *Fractured Backbones* first.

We also differentiated between mitigation of Threats and adaptation to their effects. Mitigation is the act of reducing how harmful, unpleasant, or bad something will be: it needs to be societal. Adaptation is the process of changing to suit different conditions once the effects of the Threat have happened. It may bring opportunities to society, organisations or individuals.

The second source of change are trends which are happening here and now. We call these Forces for Change. These are observable and often it is possible to have a good idea of which way they are going to develop. For instance, population growth is slowing down, with projections based on falling fertility rates.

You would probably also like to get a steer on what you can influence in all this. William MacAskill, in *What We Owe the Future*[13], argues for effective altruism and the philosophy of long-termism, "the idea that positively influencing the long-term future is a key moral priority of our time". We agree. One way that this book supports this is to provide positive glimpses of change – short stories based on real world examples about influencing the long-term future – to help you imagine what you can influence in your world and how to do it. These are positive glimpses of change, amongst the dystopia fuelled by the media!

To reduce the paralysis which can be caused by uncertainty, you can build a consistent approach to incorporating potential Threats and ongoing Forces for Change into your decision making.

The tool that we provide for this is new. It is called a Possibility Wheel. It allows you to compare decisions that you might have made under normal circumstances, with decisions informed by greater understanding of Threats and Forces for Change and how they could play out over the next 5-20 or 30 years. Throughout the book we use 'mid-term future' which is of the order of 5 years and 'long-term future' which is of the order of 20-30 years. The Possibility Wheel enables you to make more robust decisions.

Using the right tools to work with the evidence of change can help you develop resilient choices. You can then use these choices to make better decisions.

Using the book

This book has three Parts. In *Part One* we explore some of the most significant Threats that the world faces today. In *Part Two* we discuss the evidence for major Forces for Change. *Part Three* shows how to improve decision making by using the Possibility Wheel to take both Threats and Forces for Change into account.

The use of evidence and references throughout the book may appear daunting at first sight. If that is the case, we suggest you jump straight from this *Introduction* to the *Insights*. Then, if any ideas intrigue you, you can go to the chapter(s) that interest you. And working through one of the examples using the Possibility Wheel from *Part Three* can stimulate ideas for your own decision making.

Throughout the book, italicised words refer to our chapters or, if the author's name is included, it's a book.

All the chapters in *Part One* and *Part Two* include Glimpses of Change. These are chosen to be signs of positive change. But people have different ideas of what positive change is and what makes a desirable planet. We did not want to impose our views of desirability on you. So, in this book the Glimpses are of progress towards the UN Sustainable Development Goals (SDGs) for 2030 (see Appendix 1). These were developed in consultation with a wide range of stakeholders and agreed by 193 countries in 2015.

In Appendix 2 we define some terminology and list some of the primary sources of historical data and predictions from reputable bodies. Understanding the sources of data has allowed us to compare and validate projections. We find their analysis invaluable.

References (endnotes) in the text are of two types. One type of reference is to academic research and writing published in journals or other print media. The other type of reference is to signs of new phenomena emerging, or changes happening in the world – before they can be subject to academic analysis. These are often in blogs, newsfeeds or think pieces.

Where we generalise, any errors are ours. And of course, in a time of turbulent change, events may overtake the best efforts to provide up-to-date evidence.

---

[1] Susskind, D. *Growth: A reckoning*, Allen Lane, 2024

[2] Tett, G. 'Peak uncertainty on Davos' Magic Mountain', FT.com/Magazine January 21/22, 2023.

[3] Appendix 2 – Sources of Data

[4] Robinson, K. S, *The Ministry for the Future*, Orbit Books, 2020

[5] Wri.org – tinyurl.com/choices02

[6] Longfinance.net – tinyurl.com/choices01

[7] Martin Wolf, "The market can deliver the green revolution – just not fast enough", *Financial Times*, November 22, 2022 and theecoexperts.co.uk – tinyurl.com/choices03

[8] Iea.org – tinyurl.com/choices04

[9] Ritchie, H. *Not the End of the World: How we can be the first generation to build a sustainable planet,* Chatto & Windus, 2024

[10] https://ourworldindata.org/

[11] Bregman, R. *Humankind: A Hopeful History*. Bloomsbury, 2020

[12] FT.com – tinyurl.com/choices05

[13] MacAskill, W. *What We Owe the Future,* Basic Books, 2022

PART ONE – Threats

Chapter 2 – Introduction to Part One

In Part One, we explore the potential impacts of four of the major Threats facing the world in 2024. In choosing these four, we have been influenced by a number of experts. We discuss our chosen four Threats, then consider some lists of Threats identified by these experts.

To start with a definition: a Threat is "a [person or] thing likely to cause damage or danger".[1] So it isn't happening *yet*. But some Threats are already disrupting outcomes now. This means that when you consider a Threat – like the effects of *Global Heating* – it is important to consider both what is happening now *and* what could happen in the future.

Threats to society have always been with us but it is not possible to know exactly when or how they will surface. All that can be said is that they will emerge at some time, and when they do, the impact will be sudden and big. The impact will be disruptive and it is hard to anticipate what will happen and when. Our four Threats are already disrupting outcomes today. And there are likely to be further disruptions coming that are not yet observable. They are still a potential. If and when they emerge, they will be volatile and likely to cause further major changes, quickly. This means that the circumstances prevailing before the Threat arrives to disrupt the current situation are quite different from those prevailing afterwards: the Threat is a watershed.

When a Threat first surfaces, it can have an immediate impact. An example of this was the Covid-19 pandemic. People are still living with the ongoing disruptions that have flowed from that Threat (Collapse of Global Health) since it emerged and began to disrupt daily life.

Part One is organised into chapters, each describing a single Threat. Of course none of them is independent of the others; we explore them individually to make it easier to think about them.

It is important to have a clear understanding of the Threats, and which one will have the greatest impact on the decision you are planning to make, when you use the Possibility Wheel.

Four Threats

Fractured Backbones looks at how the rules of the game are (or are not) working. Backbones are agreed sets of rules which support the way that things work. Societies design these sets of rules to help people get things done.

For societies to work well – to be effective – these rules need to be shared and accepted. Then, Backbones will enable people to work, communicate and solve problems together successfully. When Backbones work well, they provide the resilience needed to adapt to other Threats.

A Backbone will have been designed for a set of circumstances. It may no longer be fit for purpose as society changes. Local Backbones may decay or become irrelevant, and it is worth noting that not all Backbones are 'good' (or good for everyone). For example, monopolies and cartels are Backbones!

Backbones may also be challenged by people who have different assumptions and therefore different sets of rules and processes. For example, different countries may have different solutions for designing a Backbone and if they want to work together, this will need addressing in order for it to work well for all. The interface between different Backbones may become a source of tension, for example as found with the Security Council of the United Nations. It isn't working as it should which means that this Backbone is fractured. When a Backbone fractures rather than evolving to fit the needs of the society, it becomes a Threat.

Fractured Backbones make it much more difficult for the world to tackle other Threats. As Sir David Omand says, "Think of experiencing a crisis as being in an unstable situation, the situation can flip either way. Good preparation allows support to be quickly available, so that a developing crisis can revert to being a manageable emergency or even being avoided altogether. But a crisis can flip the other way, sliding into disaster. Some situations cannot be pulled back and all that can be attempted is to reduce the harm done."[2]

This thinking illuminates the distinction we make between mitigation and adaptation.

Mitigation describes activities to avert global Threats and minimise impacts. These activities are often dependent on public attitudes, and they need to be implemented by governments in cooperation with one another.

Adaptation includes activities through which organisations or countries can recover from (or limit the impact from) a Threat once it has happened, or see opportunity in the new situation. This could be existing organisations adapting themselves or new organisations being formed to tackle the new situation.

The importance of Backbones in mitigation and adaptation is clear as we discuss the three remaining Threats.

Global Heating is about the climate and ecological change that the world faces. It is already a big disruptor in many parts of the planet. There are many facets to this Threat, the biggest being the uncertainty about when the changes will – or have – become irreversible, what exactly the changes will be and what (and where) their impacts will be.

In *Breakdown of International Relations,* we discuss how nations behave with one another, including trade and/or physical war. There are many factors that contribute to shifts in global order and power. While the shift may be gradual, there are often significant events that signal change.

While for much of the last century the USA was the leading power in setting the world order, this is unlikely to be so for the rest of this century. At the time of writing it seems likely that China will continue to expand its global footprint and that some middle-ranked (by GDP) countries will endure a number of wars[3].

In the world today, illness, pandemics and disease are Threats to society as well as individuals – we consider this under the broader heading of *Collapse of Global Health*. There have always been incurable, fatal infectious diseases. What is certain is that there will be another global health crisis, though we do not yet know its cause, when it will strike, or its characteristics.

The common characteristics of these four Threats are that changes in the current situation are likely to be sudden, with impacts that are difficult to imagine and plan for. There is no way to begin to predict when a further disruptive event could happen. And when it does, it disrupts the Forces for Change and any decisions that you might wish to make.

Lists of Threats

Among many books and articles on existential Threats to the society, we have been particularly influenced by four:

Ian Bremmer's *The Power of Crisis*[4] focuses on three Threats:
- Pandemic politics – (covered by us under *Collapse of Global Health*)
- Climate emergency – (covered by us under *Global Heating*)
- Disruptive technologies – (we include *AI* and *Biology* as Forces for Change, not Threats, although we cover some disruption from technology in *Fractured Backbones*).

William MacAskill's *What We Owe the Future*[5] sees four Threats:
- Climate change (*Global Heating*)
- Pandemic prevention (*Collapse of Global Health*)

- Nuclear war (we include conventional and nuclear war in *Breakdown of International Relations*)
- AI safety (*AI*)

We are more sanguine than MacAskill on the potential for AI, treating it as a Force for Change (and requiring effective regulation) but not a Threat.

Nouriel Roubini's *Megathreats*[6] is widely quoted. He thinks our world is in a polycrisis, and identifies 10 Threats:
- War among great nations or nuclear war (*Breakdown of International Relations*)
- Climate change (*Global Heating*)
- Global pandemics (*Collapse of Global Health*)
- AI destroying most jobs (we treat *AI* as a Force for Change)
- Deglobalisation and trade wars (*Fractured Backbones*)
- Debt crisis (we group the many possible failures of financial systems under *Fractured Backbones*)
- Implicit debt (ditto)
- Toxic financialisation (ditto)
- Unfunded liabilities from Social Security, Medicare through ageing (we treat *Population* as a Force for Change)
- Polarisation and partisanship in politics (we treat *Social Change* as a Force for Change)

The differences between us and Roubini are in categorisation – some of Roubini's identified Threats, we consider as Forces for Change, which society is better able to anticipate and manage.

Hamish McRae's *The World in 2050*[7] identifies forces for change and, at the end of his book, the author looks at ten things that might go wrong.
- The US political system fails to hold together (*Fractured Backbones*)
- China, India and the US mismanage their relationship (*Breakdown of International Relations*)
- Sub-Saharan Africa fails to escape from poverty (*Fractured Backbones*)
- Religious conflict (*Breakdown of International Relations*)

- Environmental degradation and climate change become irreversible (*Global Heating*)
- The long-term blow from Covid-19 and the pandemics that follow (*Collapse of Global Health*)
- The Middle East becomes truly unstable (*Breakdown of International Relations*)
- The information revolution may have a malign impact, not a beneficial one (*Fractured Backbones*)
- The threat to democracy (*Fractured Backbones*)

The UK government publishes a National Risk Register[8]. The 2023 Register is the external version of the National Security Risk Assessment, which is the government's assessment of the most serious risks facing the UK. It provides the government's updated assessment of the likelihood and potential impact of a broad range of risks that may directly affect the UK and its interests, and is a useful source if you want to explore the resilience of your organisation against a wide range of potential Threats.

Mitigation and Adaptation

For each Threat we discuss potential measures for mitigation and for adaptation. As pragmatic optimists, we look for stories of success in either mitigation or adaptation. We call these 'Glimpses of Change': case studies from around the world, of people creating opportunity in times of challenge and difficulty. Sometimes the biggest challenges create the greatest opportunities. For instance, on the back of the work done on vaccines for Covid-19, many new vaccines are being developed. A vaccine for malaria is being produced which will change lives in tropical countries[9].

We provide examples of success which may allow you to figure out why these 'Glimpses' were successful. You can reflect on what worked, what didn't and what might work in your environment or situation. What could you build upon it? What would you need to tweak? Where is *your* energy for change?

Contents of each Threat chapter

Each of the four Chapters in Part One has four headings:
- The Story so Far
- New and Emerging Factors

- Mitigation – what society can do – and glimpses of change
- Adaptation – what organisations and people can do – and glimpses of change

---

[1] UScourts.gov – tinyurl.com/choices06

[2] Omand, D. *How to Survive a Crisis*, Penguin Random House, 2023

[3] www.foreignaffairs.com – tinyurl.com/choices07

[4] Bremmer, I. *The Power of Crisis: How Three Threats – and Our Response – Will Change the World*, Simon & Schuster, 2022

[5] MacAskill. W. *What We Owe the Future*, Basic Books, 2022

[6] Roubini, N. *MegaThreats: Ten Dangerous Trends That Imperil Our Future, And How to Survive Them*, Little, Brown and Company, 2022

[7] McRae, H. *The World in 2050: How to think about the future*, Bloomsbury, 2022.

[8] Gov.uk – tinyurl.com/choices08

[9] Bbc.co.uk – tinyurl.com/choices10

Chapter 3 – Fractured Backbones

- Societies are dependent on a set of rules and shared assumptions about the way things work – these form a Backbone.
- For societies to work well, these rules need to evolve so they remain fit for purpose over time.
- Both within societies and internationally, many of these Backbones are now fracturing – that is, breaking rather than evolving.

The Story So Far

A Backbone is a set of rules which are shared, agreed and support the way that things work. Backbones can be explicit – as in being based upon the rule of law – or implicit, being based upon assumptions about 'the way we do things around here'. Societies design Backbones to enable that particular society to work well and to be effective. Backbones cover many aspects of life such as financial services, governance, health, and international (technical and professional) standards. All Backbones are based upon agreements or assumptions that the people who rely upon them make in order to get things done effectively. As we discussed the concept of Backbones across our network of friends and colleagues, we realised that most Backbones function on the foundation of an agreed upon Rule of Law.

The Western Rule of Law consists of four components[1]:

- Everyone is equal before the law
- Everyone has access to the published law
- Law is administered by an independent judiciary
- Everyone has access to justice

In "Plan on Building the Rule of Law in China (2020–2025)", the leadership in Beijing has set out its vision for a coherent legal system. The aim is to use the law to make the state more efficient and to reduce the arbitrariness of how the law is applied for the majority of the population. However, the Plan rejects an independent judiciary and the principle of separation of powers as "erroneous Western thought"[2].

The Rule of Law can be seen as the foundation of all other rights, and, without rights, nothing else works. For example, without the Rule of Law:

- There is no contract system
- There are no financial services
- There is no intellectual property so that wealth creation is stymied

There is evidence that the Rule of Law is not always observed[3]:

- Elites and countries are seen to flout the law globally
- In some parts of the world the judiciary is not independent

There is also evidence that the decay of the Rule of Law is a global phenomenon[4]. Reasons suggested for the decay of the Rule of Law include[5] democratic decay and social inequality.

We find it useful to explore the causes and effects of this decay by considering the noticeable fracturing of Backbone systems, which exposes the underlying characteristics of the Rule of Law.

Individual Backbones are designed for a set of circumstances. And circumstances change. Over time, systems of governance, trade, standards – Backbones – may become unfit for purpose. They can decay through lack of maintenance. They may become irrelevant, challenged by new conditions. When Backbones are fractured, it can mean that governments cannot respond as they need to across the range of areas in which an effective response is needed. For example, in the UK, the National Health Service is an organisation which is built on the Backbone of a set of rules which address what a health service needs to do to keep its population healthy. It is not currently succeeding in this, as is evidenced by, for instance, the rising backlog of people waiting for operations[6]. The organisation no longer effectively adheres to the Backbone upon which it was built.

Backbones and their underlying laws need to evolve over time to meet these new circumstances, to remain fit for purpose. They become a Threat when they fracture and break rather than evolve.

While local Backbones are essential to quality of life, our focus in this chapter is the Threat from the fracture of the international Backbones which have allowed societies to collaborate over the past decades. One of the challenges of this century is to maintain these Backbones – or to replace them with others – in a way that allows societies with different cultures to adapt and continue to work successfully and effectively together.

Some examples are:

- The UN and other international organisations formed after WWII (e.g. World Trade Organisation, IMF, World Bank, Asian Development Bank) are organisations which were established to sustain and enforce adherence to Backbones
- Currency exchange platforms are Backbones
- ISO standards for technology e.g. engineering components, telecommunications systems, manufactured components are Backbones
- Science and Technology Co-operation Agreement (STA) between the US and China is a Backbone

Fractured Backbones lead to breakdowns in communication, trade and international relations. They are a major Threat as we write.

New and emerging factors

Why are international Backbones in danger of fracturing?

At the meeting of the United Nations General Assembly, which began on September 19th 2023 in New York, the leaders of four of the five permanent members of the Security Council – the UN's most powerful executive body – were absent; and the organisation has been unable to do anything to prevent the invasion of Ukraine or to facilitate a ceasefire there, or in Gaza as we write. The system has apparently ground to a halt[7].

The UN continues to shape a large part of international interaction, but today there are two key areas of resistance to it. One is the emergence of countries in the Majority World challenging its implementation of the liberal order. The second is that far-right groups have been gaining greater traction across the European political spectrum and international fora, with their members often challenging international organisations and their policies. For instance, they have profoundly changed negotiations on the Global Compact for Migration in the United Nations (UN)[8].

The world is emerging into a newly multipolar system where differing worldviews co-exist. The UN is just one of the Backbones widely accepted over the past decades which are now fracturing and losing the support of the Majority World[9] (we have chosen to use the term Majority World instead of Global South because our friends and colleagues who live and work there prefer it). Organisations with a more defined focus and which evolve, do thrive and maintain their backbones – for instance, NATO.

This has come about partially through the disruptive effect of information and communications technology (ICT) in supporting the exchange of rules-based information. People in most countries have access to information now, in a way that was never possible before. So when international organisations, governments or corporations renege on a rule, it is visible to many.

The internet is supported by another international Backbone. Across the planet, in 2022 two-thirds of the population used the internet[10]. The internet depends on hardware, software and platforms, which are based on accepted rules and definitions across many different suppliers, operating in many different locations and countries. The suppliers work to agreed international standards of components – the Backbone. When there are so many different parties working together, it is easy for the Backbone to lose its fitness for purpose. This leads to it fracturing and the effects of a fracture in the internet could cripple millions of users, many countries, financial systems, and transportation systems – similar to the blocking of the Suez Canal in 2023.

This explosion of connectivity has led to new forms of financial services, entertainment and online trading – both b2b and between individuals. It has also allowed the economies of the USA and China to become interdependent, with global supply chains covering many industries. It has enabled medical and pharmaceutical research, as evidenced by the global cooperation to develop Covid-19 vaccines[11]. The resilience of digital Backbones has been the subject of concern with, for example, the UK National Preparedness Commission's report[12] which highlights the growing importance of software in the economy and society, and lack of awareness of its fragility.

A Backbone threatened with fracture by US politics is the Science and Technology Agreement (STA) – an umbrella agreement between the US and China responsible for achievements in preventing spinal birth defects, in seismology, agriculture, and many other fields[13].

The IMF and World Bank are struggling to simultaneously tackle pandemic-induced deprivation and escalating climate change-triggered needs[14]. Meanwhile, as we will see in *Economic Activity,* the power of corporations has been increasing at the expense of nation states[15]. This changes what is needed for Backbones to function properly (e.g. governance and finance), leading them to fracture.

Mitigating the impacts of fractured international Backbones is important as we face what could be existential Threats from *Global Heating*, *Collapse of Global Health*, and *Breakdown of International Relations*.

Threats turn into events – which may be a crisis. The existence of a Backbone can mean that the crisis becomes a manageable emergency. Without planning and a working Backbone to implement actions, the event can slide into disaster[16].

Mitigating the Impacts of Fractured Backbones

One of the most common patterns that has jumped out from analysis of historical patterns is how extreme inequality shows up in nearly every case of major crisis and *Fractured Backbones*. When big gaps exist between the haves and have-nots, not just in material wealth but also access to positions of power, this breeds frustration, dissent and turmoil[17]. The Backbones of the post-WWII era made assumptions about common aims such as to decrease poverty, and the methods which would achieve that[18]. Some of the aims are captured in the UN SDGs – see Appendix 1. Most of these aims are in fact shared across many cultures, with some exceptions, such as the denial of female education in Afghanistan[19]. However, there is now widespread understanding that methods of developing effectively functioning Backbones will differ across different cultures and societies, and that the world is multipolar.

In this multipolar world, some approaches seem to work better:

- Agreeing on common areas of concern and action, and organising to tackle them. One example is the Montreal Protocol, which has been ratified by every country in the world, and has been successful in phasing out ozone-depleting substances such that the ozone layer should return to pre-1960 levels by the middle of this century[20].
- Recognition of the Majority World and its problems by the global north/mature economies within the framework of international bodies. One example is the Green Revolution, which initially focused on Mexico with sponsorship from the UN and the Food and Agriculture Organisation (FAO)[21].

Glimpses of change

- NATO currently has 32 members and is an example of an institution that is upholding and maintaining a Backbone, as it is just about to celebrate its 75th anniversary. "... in terms of scope and depth of cooperation as well as longevity, NATO has no parallel anywhere."[22] It has survived the collapse of the Soviet Union and the post-Cold

War era by adjusting to the environment and system around it, by taking on other security challenges such as terrorism and piracy, and engaging in out-of-area operations as well as non-war operations.
- The ICC – International Criminal Court – is an independent judicial institution that has the authority to prosecute individuals for the most serious crimes of international concern, such as genocide, war crimes, crimes against humanity, and aggression. It has shown its teeth in issuing an arrest warrant for Vladimir Putin[23].
- "Space junk is a problem that can only be resolved internationally. Space is a shared resource – orbiting the Earth takes only around 100 minutes, and every event that generates debris in space has immediate global impacts. That's why international cooperation has been established to prevent space junk. In future, we should ensure that every mission cleans up after itself by carrying out manoeuvres at the end of the mission to remove all traces. This is the principle that the ESA is keen to introduce for its own missions from 2030."[24] A missile from a rogue nation could cause a domino effect of destruction of objects in low earth orbit to such a degree that escaping our planet for some decades to come will be impossible: a moratorium on such missile testing is now in place[25] though not all nations have signed up.
- The UK Government is addressing *Fractured Backbones* by introducing "new structures at the heart of the UK Government to focus on resilience and ensure decisions are made with an eye on the challenges we might face. The new Resilience Directorate in the Cabinet Office will drive the implementation of the measures set out in this framework and develop our ongoing resilience programme. This will include building on the National Security Risk Assessment (NSRA) to consider the chronic vulnerabilities and challenges that arise from the geopolitical and geoeconomic shifts, systemic competition, rapid technological change, and transnational challenges such as climate change, health risks and state threats that define contemporary crises."[26]

Adapting to the Impacts from Fractured Backbones

What societal or organisational characteristics might support adaptation to the fracturing of existing international Backbones? How might replacement Backbones emerge?

We can see three strands which contribute – recognition of an ongoing need and focus; a level of trust of 'others' to define the rules of law; and innovation and entrepreneurship to build new systems.

All three strands are visible in the emergence of replacement financial systems using new technology. They are arguably less visible in the emergence of the Belt and Road Initiative (BRI) launched by China in 2013 to improve connectivity and cooperation on a transcontinental scale. Funding was provided by China, although this tailed off before Covid-19. More than 150 countries have signed up[27]. BRI projects have the potential to substantially improve trade, foreign investment, and living conditions for citizens in participating countries – but only if China and other economies adopt deeper policy reforms that increase transparency, expand trade, improve debt sustainability and mitigate environmental, social and corruption risks[28]. These policy reforms are the essential requirement for this Backbone to be effective[29].

Often, Backbones replacing international agreements have a less global focus. The retreat from global supply chains to 'reshore', seen as a reaction to the fracture of supply chains during the Covid-19 pandemic, is an example[30]. Some of the hurdles to – and opportunities arising from – replacing global supply chains are discussed in a recent Institute for Manufacturing (IfM) report[31].

Glimpses of change

- Replacement Backbones in the financial system have been built on technology – for instance it is suggested that blockchain could replace SWIFT for cross-border payments[32]. And micro-banking using mobile phones is funding entrepreneurs who – in previous generations – might have tried unsuccessfully to get a bank loan[33].
- For the 70 Belt and Road (BRI) "corridor economies" (excluding China), the value of all projects already executed, in implementation, or planned, is estimated to amount to US$575 billion. If completed, BRI transport projects could reduce travel times along economic corridors by 12%, increase trade between 2.7% and 9.7%, increase income by up to 3.4% and lift 7.6 million people from extreme poverty. However, the BRI is not about making money – it is about extending influence. China wants far more than just neighbouring territory and compliant neighbours – it wants a world order with Chinese characteristics[34].

- The WTO is the body which frames trade rules: these rules are changing their focus towards encouraging trade as a way of supporting developing countries[35].
- The new president of Guatemala, Bernardo Arévalo, is going *back* to using the existing rule of law Backbone. He was elected on a strong anti-corruption platform. The institutions in Guatemala are set up such that the prosecutor general is "sort of a co-equal branch of state" entirely independent of the president. The current incumbent, Consuelo Porras, is in post until her term comes to an end in 2026. Fransisco Toro notes, "Anywhere else in Latin America, this would have been a train crash. The president would have insisted on getting rid of her, whether legally or illegally. But that's not who Bernardo Arévalo is. Bernardo Arévalo's take is that if he has to cohabitate with this figure for the first two years of his presidency, well, that's just what the law is."[36] The governance Backbone was fractured, because it was not based upon a consistent Rule of Law. This is an example of restoring the Backbone so that it would work again, and in so doing, building trust among citizens.

But the bad news is real: Russia is likely to be a problem for the long term. For the situation to change requires Russian leaders to change their minds: an unlikely event for a very long time. When Putin dies or is overthrown, there is likely to be a destabilising leadership struggle.

As the world becomes more multipolar, Backbones must adapt to remain useful. If they do not, as with all Threats, disruptions will occur.

---

[1] lexisnexis.co.uk – tinyurl.com/choices11
[2] Swp-berlin.org – tinyurl.com/choices14
[3] 'The Rule of Law is in more trouble than democracy', *Financial Times*, 31 August 2023.
[4] Lawsociety.ie – tinyurl.com/choices15
[5] Some.ox.ac.uk – tinyurl.com/choices18
[6] Bbc.co.uk – tinyurl.com/choices20
[7] Theconversation.com – tinyurl.com/choices22
[8] Cordis.europa.eu – tinyurl.com/choices25
[9] Borgenproject.org – tinyurl.com/choices26
[10] Worldbank.org – tinyurl.com/choices27
[11] Ted.com – tinyurl.com/choices28

[12] Elephant in the Room | National Preparedness Commission
[13] 'Time is running out for an old agreement about scientific research', *The Economist*, 26 August 2023
[14] 'Overlapping crises could fracture the global financial system', *Financial Times*, 7 September 2023
[15] Provost, C. and Kennard, M. *Silent Coup: How corporations overthrew democracy,* Bloomsbury, 2023
[16] Omand, D, *How to Survive a Crisis,* Penguin Random House, 2023
[17] Theconversation.com – tinyurl.com/choices29
[18] Britannica.com – tinyurl.com/choices30
[19] Unesco.org – tinyurl.com/choices31
[20] Ritchie, H, *Not the End of the World,* Penguin Random House, 2024
[21] Treehugger.com – tinyurl.com/choices32
[22] Foreignpolicy.com – tinyurl.com/choices34
[23] News.un.org – tinyurl.com/choices35
[24] Deutschland.de – tinyurl.com/choices36
[25] Spacenews.com – tinyurl.com/choices37
[26] Gov.uk – tinyurl.com/choices38
[27] 'Where to from here?', *The Economist*, 9 September 2023
[28] Worldbank.org – tinyurl.com/choices39
[29] There are also comments that some construction has been shoddy, leaving the host country to pick up the bill e.g. Wsj.com – tinyurl.com/choices40
[30] Csis.org – tinyurl.com/choices41
[31] Ifm.eng.cam.ac.uk – tinyurl.com/choices42
[32] Techtimes.com – tinyurl.com/choices43
[33] Hks.harvard.edu – tinyurl.com/choices45
[34] Noahpinion.blog – tinyurl.com/choices33
[35] Weforum.org – tinyurl.com/choices46
[36] Persuasion.community – tinyurl.com/choices47

Chapter 4 – Global Heating

- Global heating is now apparent across the globe, with highest ever average and peak temperatures being recorded in the oceans and in the atmosphere.
- Resulting changes in weather patterns are being felt differently in different parts of the world.
- Mitigation of global heating will depend on shared global agreements and actions, since the oceans and atmosphere are shared. Adaptation is often more local.

The Story So Far

The world has had extraordinary climate stability since the last Ice Age ended 11,000 years ago. This has been crucial to human development. Since the middle of the last century, however, air and sea temperatures have risen year on year, though at differing rates in different areas. So the story so far is that the global heating that we are experiencing is caused by people and their economic activity creating growing carbon emissions, which leads to global heating.

The scientific framework for understanding the cause of global heating is found in John Houghton's *Global Warming*[1]. A significant contributor is the release of pollutants (including greenhouse gases or GHGs) into the atmosphere. Initiatives to reduce global heating focus on reducing emissions of CO_2 and methane (CH_4) and developing carbon capture to reduce levels of these gases in the atmosphere.

Global heating has many effects[2], both direct and indirect. Direct effects include the melting of the ice in polar regions, rising sea levels and desertification.

The Himalayas have many of the world's glaciers, and are heating faster than other parts of the world. The loss of their glaciers has knock-on effects on the rivers and agriculture of Asia[3]. Thawing of ice in Antarctica accelerated in 2023[4]. "What's happened here is unlike the Arctic sea ice expanse", says Mark Serreze, director of the U.S. National Snow and Ice Data Center. We've come to expect a dramatic decline in sea ice at Earth's other pole, "Not much has happened to Antarctica's sea ice until the last few years. But it's just plummeted."

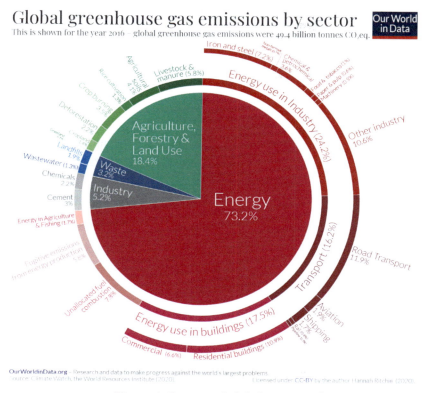

Figure 1: Sources of global emissions[5]

Oceans have been getting hotter, with surface temperatures reaching record levels for June in 2023. Parts of the North Atlantic have seen an "unprecedented" marine heat wave, with temperatures up to 5° Celsius (9° Fahrenheit) hotter than usual[6].

As water warms, it absorbs more CO_2 and becomes more acidic. Acidification is killing corals and threatening fishing while the melting of ice threatens low-lying coastal regions and coastal cities. The combination of increased temperatures and rising sea levels is an existential threat to some of the world's largest cities[7].

Global heating is causing desertification in regions across the world, threatening food supplies and leading to mass migration of populations. Average temperatures globally in 2023 were the hottest since records began[8].

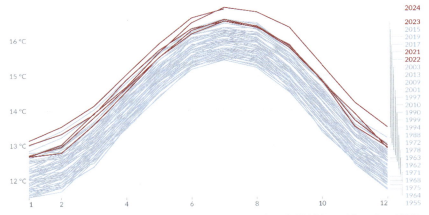

Figure 2: Earth is Heating Up[9]

Global heating is happening. The resulting extreme weather events are unpredictable in both location and timing. The world has been used to the chaotic weather caused by El Niño[10] – this will continue. The number and extent of extreme events caused by global heating are new.

More hurricanes are recorded each year as well as more extreme heat and cold. Precipitation (rain and snowfall) has increased across the globe, on average. Yet some regions are experiencing drought and unpredictable rainfall. This increases the risk of wildfires, lost crops, flooding, and drinking water shortages. In one month in 2021, record temperatures devastated the west of North America, record floods took out subway systems in China, floods in Europe left hundreds of people missing and Johannesburg in South Africa recorded the lowest temperature ever. The extreme weather, and the fires it caused in California in 2023, focused even more attention on global heating.

It is clear that reducing economic activity alone cannot reduce CO_2 levels. According to Carlo Buontempo, director of Europe's Copernicus Climate Change Service[11], "Because of the inertia in the climate system, even if we were to significantly reduce or stop our emissions today, you would still see the expected increase in temperature for the next 20 years to be almost unaffected. In reality it is very likely that the total concentration of CO_2 in the atmosphere will continue going up in the future."

What this means is that it is only over a longer period – say 50 years – that we might have a chance to start to reverse global heating. But, as MacAskill says, for the good of our grandchildren, working to make it happen is in the public interest[12]. "By averting permanent catastrophes, thereby ensuring civilisation's survival; or by changing civilisation's trajectory to make it better while it lasts ... Broadly, ensuring survival increases the quantity of future life; trajectory changes increase its quality".

New and emerging factors

Recent extreme weather, wildfires and record heat are focusing attention on attempts to reduce carbon emissions and hence long-term global heating. Meanwhile the financial costs of failing to slow the rise in global average temperatures are potentially vast and not sufficiently factored into asset values[13].

The concept of a 'green premium' can be used to estimate the costs of de-carbonising each sector. This premium is lowest for heating and cooling of buildings, which means that designing new buildings is an obvious target. Similarly, getting people to buy new electric powered passenger cars and buses is relatively easy, making these an obvious target. Conversion of other forms of transport is more difficult and expensive.

Mitigating Global Heating

The UN Climate Change Conference has been held annually (except in 2020 due to the Covid-19 pandemic) since the first UN climate agreement in 1992. International Backbones are used by governments to develop and implement policies to limit global temperature rises and adapt to impacts associated with climate change. The conference led to the first loss and damage fund being created[14]. It has looked for agreement on national targets for carbon emissions in an attempt to limit global heating. This is a severe test of international agreements and the International Backbones established by the UN. It has highlighted tensions between the Global North and the Majority World countries on "who should pay"[15].

Plan for the Planet by Ian Chambers and John Humble[16] explores how to meet the targets, describing the roles of governments, organisations and people, as well as that of technology. For instance, governments can target their international aid to reducing global heating. They could introduce small modular nuclear generation or gas-fired power stations where coal has been used before. Urban areas can create emission zones, accessible to CO_2 emitters only upon payment of a fee.

One of the measures proposed to mitigate global heating is re-forestation – planting trees. However, calculations suggest that 22 trees are needed to compensate for a typical car commute[17]. So, while there are many good reasons to plant trees, trees are only one part of tackling global heating.

Understanding the importance of different sectors of the economy has been emphasised in Bill Gates' book *How to Avoid a Climate Disaster: The solutions we have and the breakthroughs we need*[18]. About three quarters of carbon emissions come from industry (particularly the manufacture of steel and concrete), electricity generation and agriculture. The rest come from transport and from the heating and cooling of buildings.

Glimpses of Change

- Recent announcements by governments have focused on plans to achieve carbon neutrality – that is, an economy which does not emit additional carbon into the atmosphere. Xi Jinping has announced that China will achieve carbon neutrality by 2060, an important signal[19]. China added 216 GW of solar power in 2023, more than the total in place in the US (161 GW)[20, 21]. Similarly, steps in the US to invest in 'Green Tech' are planned to impact emissions by 2030[22].

- Carbfix, a start up in Iceland, is turning carbon dioxide into rocks, so that it is stored forever instead of escaping into the atmosphere[23]. It is developing two forms of technology, carbon capture and carbon removal. Carbon capture traps gas from the smokestacks of factories and power plants before it escapes into the atmosphere. This can cut a company's emissions to zero. Carbon removal withdraws CO_2 from the air and can help offset an organisation's emissions, or even make its impact negative, by taking more CO_2 out of the air than it produces.

- In June 2022, Volvo Construction Equipment became the first manufacturer in the world to deliver a construction machine built using fossil-free steel to a customer. The coking coal, traditionally needed for ore-based steel making, was replaced by renewable electricity and hydrogen[24].

- The effects of global heating have been so extreme already that some scientists are saying it is time to start geo-engineering in the sky. An approach that takes a global view is Stratospheric Aerosol Injection. To lessen sunlight worldwide by several percent, a fleet of 90 to 100 planes would fly into the stratosphere every day and release thousands of metric tons of sulphur dioxide, (the gas released by volcanoes). This would react with the stratosphere gases to form aerosols that block incoming rays[25].

- "Most of the world's population wants to fight climate change, but that majority thinks they are in the minority", says Teodora Boneva. She is a co-author of a study that asked 130,000 people in 125 countries whether they would be willing to give away 1% of their household income every month to fight global warming. 69% said yes. And 89% of respondents wished that governments would do more to tackle global warming.[26]

Adapting to Global Heating

Some aspects of global heating that society will have to adapt to include:
- As temperatures rise some areas will benefit from the ability to grow additional crops or to farm additional territory, while others suffer from desertification.
- More extreme weather – and different weather patterns – with a mostly disruptive effect.
- Rising sea levels affecting coastal cities.

Glimpses of Change

- Global heating opens up some new opportunities: the thawing of the ice in the Arctic has opened up the Northern Sea Route, connecting Asia, Russia, Europe and North America, thus shortening shipping routes. It is also becoming possible to grow crops nearer the Arctic as the planet gets warmer, the growing season lengthens, and some crop yields have improved. Yields of sorghum have increased year on year in sub-Saharan Africa and across Asia due to climate shifts since the 1970s[27]. The south of England could become one of the world's premier wine-growing regions within the next five decades[28].
- The 'Green Wall of Africa' was first proposed by a former President of Senegal, Abdouley Wade and launched in 2007[29]. Its mission is to restore plants and trees in a band running across the continent south of the Sahara. The restored landscape includes many groundwater

wells refilled with drinking water and rural towns with additional food supplies. There are new sources of work and income for villagers, thanks to work on tree maintenance. Despite ongoing difficulties in many countries across the Sahel, the increase in tree cover is visible on NASA photographs from space.

- Indonesia is planning to move its capital from Jakarta in Java to a new city named Nusantara in East Kalimantan on the island of Borneo[30]. The move is in part to relieve pressure on traffic-clogged Jakarta, which is polluted and crowded. Running alongside the news of the new capital has been news of how Jakarta is sinking into the sea, and that rising sea levels will cause chaos.

---

[1] Houghton, J, *Global Warming*, Cambridge University Press 2015
[2] For a fuller discussion of the effects of Global Heating, see Lustig, P. and Ringland, G. *New Shoots*, KDP 2021 (Out of print)
[3] Dw.com – tinyurl.com/choices48
[4] Sciencenews.org – tinyurl.com/choices49
[5] Hannah Ritchie (2020) – 'Sector by sector: where do global greenhouse gas emissions come from?' OurWorldInData.org – tinyurl.com/choices90
[6] Edition.cnn.com – tinyurl.com/choices50
[7] Timeout.com – tinyurl.com/choices51
[8] Climate.nasa.gov – tinyurl.com/choices52 & Statista – tinyurl.com/choices88
[9] ourworldindata.org – tinyurl.com/choices89
[10] 'Extreme weather – El Niño will bring chaotic weather to large parts of the world', *The Economist*, 26 August 2023.
[11] Euronews.com – tinyurl.com/choices55
[12] MacAskill, W. *What we Owe the future: A Million Year View*, Oneworld Publications, 2023
[13] *FT Big Read*: 'Climate Change', 18 August 2023.
[14] Un.org – tinyurl.com/choices56
[15] Bbc.co.uk – tinyurl.com/choices57
[16] Chambers, I. and Humble, J., *Plan for the Planet*, Routledge, 2017
[17] With special thanks to Emeritus Professor Sebastien Salibar for his calculations
[18] Gates, B. *How to Avoid a Climate Disaster: the solutions we have and the breakthroughs we need*, Allen Lane, 2021
[19] Weforum.org – tinyurl.com/choices58

[20] 'Tackling climate change: Is China laggard or pioneer', *The Week*, 19 August 2023
[21] Interestingengineering.com – tinyurl.com/choices59
[22] Ft.com – tinyurl.com/choices60
[23] *Financial Times* – 'Climate tech to save the planet: Out of thin air' and www.carbfix.com/
[24] Volvogroup.com – tinyurl.com/choices61
[25] 'A Stratospheric Gamble', Douglas Fox, *Scientific American*, October 2023
[26] 'How to do climate policy without a green backlash', *Financial Times*, 14 February 2024
[27] Frontiersin.org – tinyurl.com/choices62
[28] Independent.co.uk – tinyurl.com/choices63
[29] 'Africa's dream of a Great Green Wall dries up', *Sunday Times*, 12 March 2023
[30] Futuresoutheastasia.com – tinyurl.com/choices64

Chapter 5 – Breakdown of International Relations

- Since the time of the Greeks, societal change means that death from warfare (as a percentage of all deaths) has been falling[1].
- The world is now seeing a proliferation of 'small' wars, in addition to the global tensions between China, Russia, and The Global North.
- As technology – the use of unmanned drones – makes the destruction caused by warfare relatively risk-free for the controller, the challenge is to establish a world consensus on other methods of reaching agreements where there is conflict.

The Story So Far

This chapter is written at a time when the threat of war seems higher than at any time since the 1930s. We have tried to take a balanced view, but it needs to be emphasised that we have no privileged access to information. Hopefully a standoff and set of agreements like those made to end the Cold War will emerge from our current collection of flashpoints.

Breakdown of International Relations describes the behaviour of nations towards one another, whether it is a trade or physical war.

Wars have been a part of human history ever since nomadic tribes fought for space. Steven Pinker in *The Better Angels of Our Nature*[2] uses historical evidence to argue that there has been a dramatic reduction in violence during the past few millennia. The shift toward nonviolence, he says, has been driven by many factors, such as the spread of settled communities and the rise of feminism and democracy. The myths and metaphors of the USA and Europe (The Global North) – including feminism, democracy, Nazism, communism, nuclear weapons and colonialisation – have dominated global discourse for the past century.

Although since WWII the percentages of people dying in wars decreased, war continues to be a significant feature of international relations. Upward of 175 million people died in war-related violence during the 20th century[3]. And even in a time generally perceived as peaceful, 2011, the Stockholm International Peace Research Institute (SIPRI)[4] assessed that between 15 and 20 major armed conflicts were in progress. By 2022 this number had reached 50.

The dominance of the myths and metaphors of The Global North is unlikely to continue in this century as its relative economic power declines. There are many factors that contribute to these shifts in global order and power. Population and economic growth in Asia and more recently in Africa, have underpinned a shift in the power balance[5]. This means that different worldviews and assumptions about relationships, politics, business, and economic and social systems are informing decisions with global effect[6]. This could, in the short term, complicate the world's ability to maintain stable and peaceful international relations, across differing rules of law.

One of the effects that is noticeable is the decline in the credibility of the UN Security Council in peacekeeping[7]. Other UN bodies, such as the General Assembly or the Economic and Social Council with different membership, could move centre stage on matters of peace and security.

Another effect is the spread of weapons of mass destruction – conventional, nuclear, and biological – that can affect whole populations[8]. Many of these are now under the control of a person or small group with unchecked power. Missile tests in North Korea and bioweapons in Syria are examples[9,10].

The link between food insecurity, political upheaval, social instability, and conflict is well established[11]. Initially, the war in Ukraine drove up world food and energy prices, contributing to a widespread cost-of-living crisis[12].

We observe that international relations (as we write) are breaking down, and this threatens to hamper efforts to maintain Global Health and attempts to mitigate Global Heating. The decreased functionality of many international Backbones is both a cause and an effect. *Fractured Backbones* can lead to proxy wars, for example Iran's concern about changing relations in the Middle East leading to the proxy war through Hamas with Israel.[13]

New and emerging factors

While the shift in balance of power may be gradual, there are often significant and unexpected events that signal change. For instance, it was unexpected that China would broker a truce between Iran and Saudi Arabia[14]; NATO has been unexpectedly strengthened by Russia's invasion of Ukraine, gaining its 31st member (Finland) in April 2023[15] and its 32nd member[16] (Sweden) in February 2024; and Europe's energy profile has been unexpectedly re-configured to cope with the reduced supply of Russian oil and gas[17]. Hamas's attack on Israel in 2023 was largely unexpected when it occurred[18]. These unexpected events could signal a change in the pattern of international relations from the last century.

In particular, China as a global force, with investments in the Belt and Road Initiative (BRI)[19] across every continent and the ability to broker truces outside Asia, signals a new era. This is an era in which it becomes important for the Global North and China to find ways of cooperating on global issues such as Global Heating, and to agree to disagree where there are differences, as Reagan and Gorbachev did in 1986. The two leaders recognised in each other the desire to move past tense politics and end a nuclear standoff[20]. The approach was to agree on an area where they could – and needed to – work together.

Information and Communication Technology (ICT) has an increasingly significant role. Disinformation is not new[21], but social media platforms have ramped up the circulation of real and false images. Drones have become much more visible recently in physical warfare. Cybercrime is estimated to cost the world $10.5 trillion annually by 2025[22], with cyber warfare estimated to cost about 10% of that[23].

Weapons of mass destruction have been available to a number of governments but were unused for several decades – this restraint may not continue. It is to be hoped (as we write) that verbal threats made by autocrats will not be carried out[24].

Mitigating the Breakdown of International Relations

In 1996, columnist Thomas Friedman proposed the Golden Arches Theory of Conflict Prevention[25], that "countries with middle classes large enough to sustain a McDonald's have reached a level of prosperity and global integration that makes warmongering risky and unpalatable to its people." Unfortunately, since the first McDonald's in Belgrade (capital of Serbia) was opened on 24 March 1988, a number of inter-ethnic conflicts have reared up across the Balkans[26] involving Serbia, although these have been localised.

More seriously, there is an opportunity to find contexts in which the USA and China face a common cause and to create a framework to tackle it in an area which affects them both, such as Global Heating.

What is often not as visible is the background work of understanding root causes and consensus-building in order to reduce the grounds for war. A report from SIPRI, *Environment of Peace: Security in a New Era of Risk*[27], surveys the evolving risk landscape and documents a number of pathways to solutions: in international law and policy, in peacekeeping operations, and among non-governmental organisations (NGOs). We discussed the role of frameworks and international agreements in *Fractured Backbones*.

Glimpses of Change

- Women Waging Peace Network[28] is a network of more than 1,000 women peacemakers from conflict areas around the world. The Network was launched in 1999 to connect these women with each other and with policy shapers. Members of the Network are elected and appointed government officials, directors of NGOs and movements in civil society, scholars and educators, businesspeople, representatives of multilateral organisations, and journalists. With varied backgrounds, perspectives, and skills, they bring a vast array of expertise to the peace-making process. The Network now resides at the Joan B. Kroc Institute for Peace and Justice (Kroc IPJ) at the University of San Diego.
- The Montreal Protocol[29] of 1987 is a treaty designed to protect the ozone layer. Ozone depletion was the first human threat to the global atmosphere to be addressed by the international community. The results have been truly remarkable. The Montreal Protocol has fulfilled its original objective by putting the stratospheric ozone layer on the road to recovery. But its effects have not stopped there: it has also done more than any other measure to date to combat climate change. And it has achieved all this through a united, indeed unanimous, world community. The Protocol is the first and only treaty ever to have been ratified by every nation on Earth. This has happened not just once, but six times over, including the underlying framework convention, the protocol, and its four amendments. The ozone layer is healing and it is likely to recover over the next decades.
- A knowledge partnership between the Stockholm International Peace Research Institute (SIPRI)[30] and the World Food Program (WFP)[31] provides an evidence base for the relationship between food and security (wars). It has proposed food-based policies to reduce conflict in Nigeria and the Central American Dry Corridor, and in South Sudan.

Adapting to the Breakdown of International Relations

Some people or organisations adapt to the *Breakdown of International Relations* into war or the threat of war, by profiteering or providing goods to underground economies. This has negative connotations and sadly, is unlikely to stop.

Resilience is the capacity to recover quickly from difficulties, and has come back onto the agenda for countries and organisations after comparative neglect during benign times, as part of adaptation to increased international tension. One of the developments after the Russian invasion of Ukraine was the emergence and celebration of a strong Ukrainian culture, with a shared narrative and amazing resilience.

Another has been the crucial role of drones, and the pace of change in their development. In 2022 Ukraine had seven domestic drone manufacturers and in 2023 it had at least eighty[32]. According to the Council on Foreign Relations, "This conflict has demonstrated the battlefield advantages of drones, which have become smaller, more lethal, easier to operate, and available to almost anyone. They shorten the time from when a target is detected to when it is destroyed, and they can bolster a military's ability to reconnoitre the battlefield. Drones with longer endurance profiles can effectively conduct hours of reconnaissance, enabling other drones to carry out precision strikes deep inside enemy territory. Other models enable individual soldiers to monitor adversary movement without risking lives or giving up the soldier's position."

Drones can also play an important international humanitarian role, for instance, by conducting battle and collateral damage assessments or exposing war crimes. Drones with high-resolution cameras will be used to help Ukraine document potential Russian war crimes. Images captured will be used to aid the Office of the Prosecutor General in documenting instances of human rights abuses.

In his book, *War Made New*[33], Max Boot, provides four lessons about adaptation in response to warfare:

- One of the things that makes innovation so tricky is that when an innovative technology arises, nobody is quite sure what to do with it. As an example, it was decades after initial naval battles with iron ships that it was realised that their winning feature was to enable enormous ships with devastating firepower, something not possible with wooden ships. The adaptation we see now is the use of drones to transform battlefields and enact decapitating strikes on hierarchies. In principle they do not need to be remotely guided – inertial guidance systems such as used in ICBMs is a solvable miniaturisation problem. What else might be possible? How do you guard against it?

- First movers are often considered to have advantages because they have a head start. However, their view of the potential available is often biased by early, unreliable versions and a lack of complementary technologies. Second movers, on the other hand, can see new possibilities. The example from warfare is the development and use of tanks – first by the UK and later used to more effect by Germany.
- Today, many militaries operate by the doctrine of commander's intent, in which the lower ranks are given specific objectives and figure out how to achieve them on their own. He notes that the corporate world (and observers add, the Russian military) has not caught up.
- Many promising young companies that focus on coming up with the 'next big thing' fail to scale it sufficiently. On the other hand, efficient operators can often capitalise on innovations developed elsewhere. Boot suggests that the decisive advantage that won World War II was the assembly line.

Glimpses of Change

- In March 2020, the World Health Organisation declared that the Covid-19 virus had developed into a global pandemic. Most experts thought that an optimistic timescale for a vaccine was 18-24 months. But within 10 months, vaccines had been developed, gone through clinical trials and regulatory approval and were being administered to individuals. There was global collaboration among scientists: the paper detailing the Oxford/Astra Zeneca vaccine had 600 authors listed. There was collaboration between different companies and between companies and universities. People worked across organisations to enable quicker progress, sometimes in teams enabled or helped by governments[34].
- The Pre-Trial Chamber of the UN-backed International Criminal Court (ICC) issued an arrest warrant for President Vladimir Putin of Russia in March 2023 in connection with alleged war crimes. It

states that he is "allegedly responsible for the war crime of unlawful deportation" of children from occupied territories in Ukraine to Russia. "The crimes were allegedly committed in Ukrainian occupied territory at least from 24 February 2022."[35] But since it is difficult to imagine that Putin could be incarcerated, lack of implementation behind the rule of law is perhaps one reason for people holding the ICC in disrespect.

---

[1] Pinker, S, *The Better Angels of Our Nature: Why Violence Has Declined*, Viking Adult, 2011
[2] Ibid
[3] Scientificamerican.com – tinyurl.com/choices65
[4] https://www.sipri.org/
[5] See later Chapters on *Population* and *Economic Activity*
[6] sharing.org – tinyurl.com/choices66
[7] globalcitizen.org – tinyurl.com/choices67
[8] rand.org – tinyurl.com/choices68
[9] time.com –tinyurl.com/choices91
[10] armscontrol.org – tinyurl.com/choices92
[11] sipri.org – tinyurl.com/choices93
[12] archive.md – tinyurl.com/choices72
[13] persuasion.community – tinyurl.com/choices94
[14] foreignpolicy.com – tinyurl.com/choices74
[15] rand.org – tinyurl.com/choices75
[16] edition.cnn.com – tinyurl.com/choices76
[17] reuters.com – tinyurl.com/choices77
[18] aljazeera.com – tinyurl.com/choices78
[19] chathamhouse.org – tinyurl.com/choices95
[20] Bremmer, I. *The Power of Crisis*, Simon and Schuster, 2022
[21] The long history of disinformation during war | Department of History (cornell.edu) – tinyurl.com/choices352
[22] cybersecurityventures.com – tinyurl.com/choices97
[23] imarcgroup.com – tinyurl.com/choices129
[24] reuters.com – tinyurl.com/choices99
[25] ft.com – tinyurl.com/choices100
[26] snopes.com – tinyurl.com/choices133
[27] sipri.org – tinyurl.com/choices132

[28] inclusivesecurity.org – tinyurl.com/choices134
[29] unep.org – tinyurl.com/choices130
[30] https://www.sipri.org/
[31] sipri.org – tinyurl.com/choices131
[32] cfr.org – tinyurl.com/choices135
[33] Boot, M. *War Made New: Technology, warfare and the course of history*, 1500 to the present day, Gotham Books, 2007
[34] Lustig, P. and Ringland, G. *New Shoots*, KDP, 2021. (out of print)
[35] news.un.org – tinyurl.com/choices136

Chapter 6 – Collapse of Global Health

- The Covid-19 pandemic showed the power of innovation under pressure, sharing information globally to quickly develop vaccines.
- The world should not assume that all future pandemics will be as treatable – it was lucky that several viruses related to Covid-19 had been seen in the preceding decades.
- In some places, industrial pollution is undoing the health gains made through improved public health measures.

The Story So Far

In the world today, illness, pandemics and disease are a threat to society as well as individuals – we consider the potential effects of this under the broader heading of the *Collapse of Global Health*.

There have always been incurable, fatal infectious diseases. Pandemics have triggered vast societal change and spurred innovation as societies tried to avoid the effects or to adapt to them.

For instance, the Black Death was a bubonic plague pandemic in Europe and North Africa from 1346 to 1353. It is the most fatal pandemic recorded in human history, causing the deaths of 75-200 million people or about one in three of the population. The massive reduction of the workforce meant their labour was suddenly in higher demand[1]. For many Europeans, while the population was depleted, there was a golden age of prosperity and new opportunities. Land was plentiful, wages high and serfdom all but disappeared.

A century ago, the flu epidemic of 1918 swept the globe, killing as many as one in 20 of the world's population — before social distancing helped curb its spread. In the early 1780s, smallpox ravaged the American West, ripping through indigenous communities with fatality rates of two in five people and leading to the development of the world's first vaccine less than two decades later.

Other outbreaks – from cholera in the 1830s to HIV-AIDS in the 1980s – brought xenophobia (and homophobia in the case of HIV-AIDS) along with disease, and history shows that fear and blame can distract from efforts to contain the infection[2].

History also shows that pandemics occur repeatedly, even if there are decades between occurrences. In 2006 leading epidemiologists stated that if pandemics stop occurring regularly then something more fundamentally worrying is happening to the planet[3]. This suggests that the world should be better prepared.

The current Covid-19 pandemic continues as we write in 2024, as the virus mutates and re-infects populations. Up to 2023, the death rate globally was estimated to be about seven million deaths, or one in 1,000 of the world's population[4]. The story of innovation to develop one of the Covid-19 vaccines is something to be optimistic about[5]; these vaccines were the reason that the death rate was so low.

Antimicrobials – including antibiotics, antivirals, antifungals and antiparasitics – are medicines used to prevent and treat infections in humans, animals and plants. Misuse and overuse of antimicrobials are the main drivers in the development of drug-resistant pathogens. Lack of clean water and sanitation and inadequate prevention and control of infection promotes the spread of microbes, some of which can be resistant to antimicrobial treatment. The cost of antimicrobial resistance (AMR) to the economy is significant.

The World Health Organization (WHO) has declared that increasing AMR is one of the top ten global public health Threats facing humanity.

The Institute for Health Metrics and Evaluation has identified eleven global health issues[6]. These include Long Covid, mental health, impact of climate change, cardiovascular disease, respiratory infections caused by influenza, poverty, diabetes, road injuries, dementia and population ageing. The list of issues also includes what we have referred to as *Fractured Backbones*:

> "Strengthening health systems globally remains a critical aspect of what is needed for resilient health systems. This will be particularly relevant as countries refocus their resources and attention after the acute phase of the Covid-19 pandemic.
>
> I think what is needed is a longer-term commitment from donors and governments – financial and human resources, governance structures, management, information systems – to ensure that interventions are set up for long-term sustainability and can deliver the outcomes that are aspired to across health systems."
>
> **Angela Micah, assistant professor and co-lead of the development assistance for health resource tracking team.**[7]

New and emerging factors

AMR affects humans, animals, the environment and the food chain. This means that fewer and fewer antibiotics work[8]. It can take 10-15 years and over $1 billion to develop a new antibiotic. However, there are some successes: recently a new drug for TB started evaluation[9]. And scientists have discovered an entirely new class of antibiotic that is a possible solution to AMR. "Zosurabalpin defeated highly drug-resistant strains of Carbapenem-resistant *Acinetobacter baumannii* (Crab) in mouse models of pneumonia and sepsis, and was being tested in human trials."[10] There haven't been any new antibiotics approved for Gram-negative bacteria in more than 50 years.

We could encounter a new disease (termed 'Disease X') that appears seemingly from nowhere, just like Covid-19. This could be a zoonotic disease that has crossed from animals to humans.

Fungal infections are a silent threat[11]. Annually, over 150 million severe cases of fungal infections occur worldwide, resulting in approximately 1.7 million deaths per year. These numbers are increasing each year. Additionally, the long-term therapeutic application and prophylactic use of antifungal drugs in high-risk patients have promoted the emergence of (multi) drug-resistant fungi, including the extremely virulent strain *Candida auris*. Hence, fungal infections are already a global threat that is becoming increasingly severe.

There are no guarantees, despite the development and work on biological technology, that we will always be able to find a cure for a pandemic.

Pandemics have societal as well as personal costs. They disrupt lifestyles, food supply chains, health and education, and working patterns. As people's lifestyles change, the demand for transport, for electricity, for office and warehouse space all change. The electricity grid may struggle to deliver to the new location of demand.

The *Collapse of Global Health* is a very visible example contributing to *Fractured Backbones*. It disrupts the forces for change and any decisions that you might wish to make.

Mitigating the Collapse of Global Health

What societal characteristics might limit the *Collapse of Global Health*?
- Existence of functioning, effective international Backbones – of scientists, of public health, of medical experts.

- Ability to recognise the cause and detect the *Collapse of Global Health* early, through sharing health data globally.[12]
- Ability to enforce isolation of regions, towns or groups of people.
- Ability to organise medical resources to identify remedies or preventions.
- Cease automatically feeding antibiotics to animals.[13]
- End blaming the sick – it delays the ability to organise medical resources to tackle the source and so increases the number affected.

Glimpses of Change

- Malaria Vaccines[14]: A malaria vaccine with "world-changing" potential has been developed by scientists at the University of Oxford. The vaccine was recently rolled out after trials showed up to 80% protection against the deadly disease. Crucially, say the scientists, their vaccine is cheap and they already have a deal to manufacture more than 100 million doses a year. The charity 'Malaria No More' said recent progress meant the death of children from malaria could end "in our lifetimes".
- There has been significant lowering of the infant mortality rate since 1990[15]. The global under-5 mortality rate has dropped by 59%, from 93 deaths per 1,000 live births in 1990 to 38 in 2021. However, children face differing chances of survival based on where they are born: sub-Saharan Africa and southern Asia account for more than 80% of the 5 million under-5 deaths in 2021, and a child born in sub-Saharan Africa is 11 times more likely to die in the first month of life than a child born in Australasia.
- The importance of handwashing, masking, cleaning and using disinfectants to prevent coronavirus infection was positively reflected in the declining incidence of intestinal infections, influenza, influenza-like illnesses, and acute respiratory infections in Mongolia[16].
- The World Health Organization (WHO) has published a report about the Southeast Asia region over the last decade (WHO call it 'The Platinum Decade'). They note that public health in these countries over the last decade now resembles that of the USA or EU, having moved from a need to focus on the diseases of poverty, to health risks associated with "poor diet and obesity, and lifestyle

choices like drinking and smoking." They note that Noncommunicable Diseases (NCDs) like diabetes, heart disease, and cancer now account for two thirds of all deaths in the region[17].

Adapting to Collapse of Global Health

What societal or organisational characteristics might support adaptation to the *Collapse of Global Health*? We observed the following adaptations during the Covid-19 pandemic:

- Organisations expedited their use of technology to make employees and customers' lives easier and better[18].
- Airlines shifted from carrying passengers to carrying freight (see Glimpses of Change: Commercial Airlines).
- Retailers adapted by offering delivery and roadside (Click & Collect) services.
- Rethinking of education and community using technology instead of physical presence (see Glimpses of Change: APF).

Glimpses of Change

- Commercial Airlines[19]: With an unprecedented drop in commercial passengers during the Covid-19 pandemic, airlines cancelled up to 90% of their scheduled flights. But instead of flying people, large airlines like Virgin Atlantic, Lufthansa, United and American Airlines, among others, instead switched to cargo-only flights. The airlines used the empty passenger cabins to transport much-needed items, including grocery items and healthcare provisions.
- APF: Collaborate 2020 was the international conference of the Association of Professional Futurists. This 'unconference' ran virtually and it was specifically designed to keep as many of the advantages of a face-to-face conference as possible, while remaining safe for participants. It was run across 20 time zones over four days, using Zoom for the virtual sessions and Miro (a virtual whiteboard and flip chart) to support each session. Previously, conferences were often hosted in the USA. In 2018 there were 70 participants with a handful from outside North America. 120 individuals took part in Collaborate 2020, with more than half based outside the USA. This helped to change the culture of the APF organisation.

[1] Hilton, R.H., *The English Peasantry in the Late Middle Ages*, Clarendon, 1974
[2] colorado.edu – tinyurl.com/choices146
[3] From a private conversation between Joe Little and Daniel Sharp, shared by Joe Little.
[4] https://www.worldometers.info/coronavirus/
[5] Lustig, P. and Ringland, G. *New Shoots*, KDP, 2021. (out of print)
[6] healthdata.org – tinyurl.com/choices137
[7] Ibid
[8] thelancet.com – tinyurl.com/choices138
[9] ucl.ac.uk – tinyurl.com/choices139
[10] theguardian.com – tinyurl.com/choices140
[11] ncbi.nlm.nih.gov – tinyurl.com/choices141
[12] https://www.who.int/data/gho
[13] ncbi.nlm.nih.gov – tinyurl.com/choices147
[14] bbc.co.uk – tinyurl.com/choices148
[15] who.int – tinyurl.com/choices142
[16] researchgate.net – tinyurl.com/choices143
[17] theprogressnetwork.org – tinyurl.com/choices144
[18] forbes.com – tinyurl.com/choices145
[19] as note 7.

PART TWO – Forces for Change

Chapter 7 – Introduction to Part Two

In Part Two we discuss major Forces for Change.

The Forces for Change we describe are trends. These are qualitatively different from Threats. They are not a fad or fleeting fashion – we are not discussing fashion trends. They are happening here and now and their outcomes are neither positive nor negative. They are observable and often it is possible to have a good idea of which way they are going to develop. For instance, population growth is slowing down as evidenced by data on fertility rates and projections. Trends will build or fade over time[1], so their progress can be tracked – and sometimes influenced.

As you work through Part Two, you will find that we have assessed widely held assumptions against evidence – for instance, on population projections. Where events have overtaken these assumptions, we explain how. We bring together the results of analysis and inputs from a wide range of experts, to assemble a more coherent story than is possible from any single silo or discipline.

Each chapter in Part Two explores one Force for Change, like *Population* or *Energy Choices*. Clearly this is simplistic. Forces for Change are not independent of each other. But we have found that discussing the Forces separately helps people and teams to frame their ideas. It provides a model of the world. Remember though, as the famous G.P. Box said, "all models are wrong, but some are useful". We have found that mere mortals (like us) find this model useful.

We have evolved and tested our selection of Forces for Change over the last decade. We have worked with many organisations and asked the question, 'What else?' in order to explore the scope of Forces for Change. We know that no single selection of Forces for Change will accurately reflect the complex global ecosystem. Mostly, we find that what is important to people is within one of our existing forces. But ... all choices of (only) a few Forces to represent the global ecosystem should be challenged! See our choices as a starting point, for you to use and build upon.

We have developed a story line – a narrative – building up a picture of the forces changing our world, starting with the world's population.

Population describes how many people there are, where the population is decreasing and where it is increasing. The challenges of declining population and longevity are already being felt in many parts of the world.

One of the biggest changes in the last century was people moving to cities from rural areas. Urban life is the dominant mode now. *Urban Pull* changes lifestyles through improved education, healthcare and employment opportunities. Awareness of pandemics is likely to force changes to urban life, as people place more importance on public health, clean air and green spaces.

This new, urban, world has developed a dependence on fossil fuels (described in *Energy Choices*) and on travel and transport (explored in *Mobility*). As we noted in the *Introduction*, electricity generated from renewables was by December 2022 cheaper than that from fossil fuels[2]: this changes mindsets and geopolitics. So, the energy used in transport is changing from fossil fuels, while lifestyle changes are reducing the amount – and changing the purpose – of travel and transport.

The world has become a *Connected World* based on computers, a multiplicity of devices and networks. The positive and negative social and economic implications of this are far reaching.

AI and robots already outperform humans in a range of applications, while the weaknesses are becoming apparent – algorithms reinforce existing biases, and false results are not easily checked. As we write, governments are discussing how to effectively regulate the application of AI.

In the next decade, the approaches described in *Connected World, AI* (Artificial Intelligence) and *Biology* could allow the world to reduce its dependence on fossil fuels, the pollution from travel and transport, and tackle the looming effects described in *Planetary Limits*. As optimists, we see a precedent in the Green Revolution, which revolutionised food supplies worldwide. Advances in *Biology* are now revolutionising human, animal and plant health at an amazing rate – which will accelerate over the next decade.

People move to cities to improve their access to education, health care, and work. The downside is that many cities in the Majority World have polluted air and poor water quality[3].

Economic Activity tells the story of how the world – particularly Asia – has seen people's living standards improving. When people are able to make choices, quality of life becomes more important.

Meanwhile, the increased role of IT-enabled platforms is changing skill needs in many industries and developing a gap between high and low earners, with increased inequality. It is increasing the potential for remote working, particularly tapping into skills in countries with educated people. The economy today is very different from that in the last century, with disruptive social effects.

One result of the Covid-19 pandemic was to provide a role model for international cooperation to tackle big problems, in the amazing feat of developing vaccines at pace. Another has been to accelerate a rethinking of value systems and the nature of work and the family, with new social structures emerging to replace those that are fragmenting. Politics and leadership, both national and international, are already changing. We explore this in *Social Change*.

Threats will blast across all the Forces for Change in a way that is difficult to plan for. We have attempted to capture the most important Threat to each Force for Change in each of the chapters in Part Two.

At the end of Part Two is a Chapter called *Pulling it all together* – that is what it does!

Optimists look for stories of success. We call these 'Glimpses of Change' in this book. Glimpses of Change are case studies from around the world in which people have created opportunity in times of challenge and difficulty. As noted in Part 1, sometimes the biggest challenges create the greatest opportunities. On the back of the work done on vaccines for Covid-19, many new vaccines are being developed. A vaccine for malaria has been produced which will change lives in tropical countries[4].

We provide examples of success which allow you to figure out why these Glimpses of Change were successful. You can reflect on what worked, what didn't and if that might work in your organisation or environment. What could you build upon it? What would you need to tweak? Where is your energy for change?

Each of the chapters describing a Force for Change has the headings:
- The Story so Far
- Glimpses of Change

Lists of Forces for Change

Many organisations work with lists of Forces for Change that they find useful for their specific business environment. The list we use can be mapped against these or other lists – as an example we referred to Hamish McRae's book earlier, here are his five Forces for Change from *The World in 2050*[5]. (Our corresponding chapters are in italic in brackets).
- Demography (*Population*)
- Resources and the Environment (*Global Heating* from Part One, *Planetary Limits, Urban Pull, Energy Choices* from Part Two)
- Trade and Finance (*Economic Activity, Mobility* from Part Two)

- Technology Races Onwards (*AI, Connected World, Biology* from Part Two)
- How Governments – and Governance – will Shift (*Social Change* from Part Two, *Collapse of International Relations* from Part One)

We hope that you find our list a useful starting point for exploring the Forces for Change affecting your organisation.

---

[1] managementtoday.co.uk – tinyurl.com/choices110
[2] theecoexperts.co.uk – tinyurl.com/choices112
[3] sciencedirect.com – tinyurl.com/choices113
[4] bbc.co.uk – tinyurl.com/choices149
[5] McRae, H. *The World in 2050: How to think about the future.* Bloomsbury, 2022.

Chapter 8 – Population

- The global population growth is reducing faster than you think.
- Women are having fewer children on average and there is an increasing proportion of older people.
- Many countries in the Global North (and some in the Majority World) have a shrinking workforce supporting a growing number of older people[1].

The story so far

For centuries population has been increasing. Our story explains why and *how* the future is different.

Since the 1970s, much of the thinking about the number of people in the world has been similar to that built into the classic *Limits to Growth*[2] which predicted a peak of 10 or 11 billion people and was concerned with the capacity to feed everybody. This trajectory was similar to the UN 2019 medium line in Figure 3 **Global population forecasts** below.

Today there is much evidence that global population is going to plateau and then decrease by mid-century, much earlier than previously predicted.

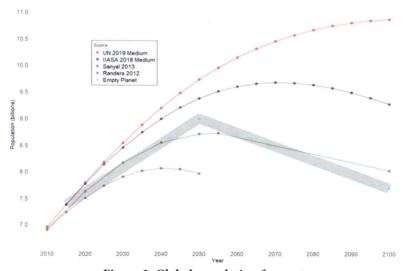

Figure 3: Global population forecasts

The differences in the forecasts shown in the graph are mostly due to differences in assumptions about fertility rates (the number of children each woman will bear), rather than assumptions about longevity.

What has happened to reduce fertility? Population is still growing in many developing economies, with the highest birth rates in rural areas. However, as families move to urban areas, in general their standard of living, and women's access to education, healthcare and employment, all improve. Within just one generation of urban living, the average number of children in a family often decreases.

Even in India, the fertility rate in 2022[3] was 2.1%, the defined replacement rate for a population. It is below the replacement rate in many countries[4]. Much of the uncertainty in the forecasts relates to the speed with which Africa becomes urban, with the corresponding drop in the birth rate.

Some seminal research on a number of indicators in India and in Kerala (a state in India with nearly universal literacy) strongly suggested that female literacy – rather than economic factors – was the main predictor for family size.

The comparative fertility rates in the data from India and Kerala illustrate the global phenomenon: other parts of the world are now experiencing what happened in Kerala. As women become literate, they have fewer children (see *Urban Pull* for another factor – moving to cities). The net effect is that in many countries, the number of children being born is less than the number of people dying. So, the population in those countries is decreasing.

Effect of Women's Education[5] Comparison of fertility rates with female literacy in India as a whole and in Kerala, illustrates the effect of literacy among women. Kerala is in most ways similar to the rest of India, but unusually its state government instituted a policy of universal literacy. The effect is shown in the table below – female literacy correlates with better life expectancy and a lower fertility rate. Life expectancy and fertility in the USA are similar to that in Kerala[6], as is female literacy – which suggests that female literacy and education could be the causal factor[7].

Data for year 2000	India	Kerala
Total fertility per woman	2.9	1.7
Infant mortality	58	12
Male life expectancy years	62	71
Female life expectancy years	64	76
Female literacy	54	88

One effect of the decline in fertility is that globally there are already more people aged 65 or over than aged five or under[8]. Firms and governments in many parts of the world are starting to plan for this. In North America, birth rates are declining[9]. Many countries in Europe and Latin America are seeing populations decline and becoming older, as are China, Russia and South Korea.

Population is affected by death rates as well as birth rates. The chart in **Figure 4: Life expectancy** shows that, in all parts of the planet, as health and living standards improve, people are living longer. Average life expectancy at birth has increased steadily from 46 in 1950 to over 72 now[10].

Though increased longevity is a worldwide trend, the ratio of old people to young people differs by country, with extreme ratios occurring in parts of Asia and, at the other end of the spectrum, in Africa. The infographic in **Figure 5: Japan and Nigeria 2040** charts the number of males and females[11, 12], in 5-year age brackets from 0-100, projected for 2040, in those countries. It shows few young people in Japan in 2040 and many people aged around 70. In Nigeria, young people are expected to dominate the population. The consequences of these differences are discussed in *Economic Activity*.

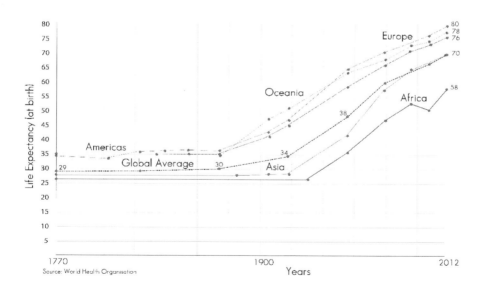

Figure 4: Life Expectancy

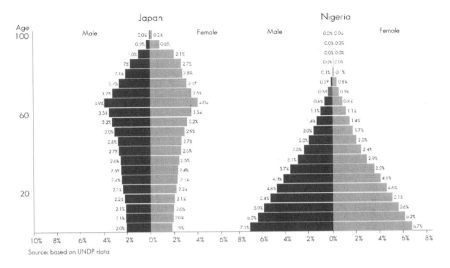

Figure 5: Japan and Nigeria 2040

Today, there are more people over the age of 100 than ever before. As Camilla Cavendish points out in *Extra Time*[13], our systems are lagging behind this reality. The new challenge in many parts of the world may well be to rethink the economies and policies of governments and their health and education systems for a declining and ageing population. Some countries, like Japan, are already facing this challenge. Meanwhile, scientists and investors are working towards the norm of a healthy life to age 120[14].

As populations have greater proportions of older people, the management and treatment of chronic disease increases in importance. The World Health Organization (WHO) has described an invisible epidemic of non-communicable (often chronic) diseases such as diabetes, heart disease, dementia and arthritis[15]. These are now responsible for over half of deaths. As chronic diseases need medication taken over long periods, public health authorities are becoming concerned about long-term effects. And it has become important to test the effects of drugs with different target populations (e.g. different genders, ages and ethnic groups).

Mental illnesses are increasingly recognised globally as diseases. The WHO indicates that by 2030 depression will be the leading cause of economic burden of disease globally[16].

Though public health advances have radically reduced the number of people killed by contagious diseases, the Covid-19 pandemic demonstrates that trade, leisure travel and migration continue to spread diseases. The question of whether – and how much – health care is a societal good or a private matter is raised again by the pandemic and societies' answers will be framed by people's experience of it. One positive effect of the pandemic has been strengthened scientific collaboration on health threats.

People are living longer so they expect to be healthy and active for longer. It is likely that there will be more older people able and wanting (or needing) to work and to make a contribution to their community. In Glimpses of Change below, we include examples of people working and staying active in sport in what used to be considered 'old age', over age 80.

These demographic shifts mean that there is also an increased need for lifelong learning due to longevity. Workers over retirement age will rarely be working at the jobs for which they initially trained forty or more years before or, if the jobs have the same name, the range of skills needed is likely to be different. Think about how a doctor's skills have had to change: forty years ago, a doctor did not have a computer or smartphone sitting on their desk. Further education will become normal even when a person stays in the same profession, and essential for those who are looking at second or third careers.

The effect of women having fewer children, combined with increased longevity, is to change family make-up. What has been seen as a typical family of three or four children, two parents and maybe two surviving grandparents is changing: families of great grandparents, grandparents, parents and one or two children may become typical. This will mean fewer children to support older generations.

Male births have always been more than half of all births, with a higher death rate in early years. Public health improvements worldwide have increased the number of surviving males so that, in 2017, less than half the world's population were women. Selective abortion further skews the ratio[17] – for instance in India 111 boys are born for every 100 girls. Across China and India, this means a surplus of 70 million men[18] – called 'incels' – men who are involuntarily celibate[19]. What might happen when the gender balance becomes so uneven? There is growing evidence[20] that many countries in Asia have become sources for a brutal business – the trafficking of women and girls for sale in China as brides.

A major change in *Population* is the effect of reduced family size and improved medicine. Together they signal a planet with a smaller population, and a historically higher proportion of older people. While all of the four Threats could slow the pace of population decline, none are thought to be likely to cause the trend to change direction towards population growth.

Glimpses of Change

Effects of declining population

- One way for a country to counter declining population is to encourage immigration of young workers of childbearing age. Countries like the USA and Canada have built their population through immigration[21]. Canada publishes lists of the 10 most successful immigrants, which include Mike Lazardis, founder of Blackberry, Rola Dagher, President of Cisco Systems Canada and Susur Lee, credited as "One of the Top Ten Chefs of the Millennium"[22].

Longevity

- De Hogeweyk is a gated model village in Weesp, The Netherlands. Designed specifically as a pioneering care facility for elderly people with dementia, its approach focuses on factors that support human health and wellbeing. It is a self-contained, enclosed village where people can shop, cook and live together safely. Basic routines and rituals can help residents maintain a better quality of life[23].
- Longevity allows people to continue to contribute their talent and wisdom to the world. There are many role models. Benjamin Zander clearly enjoys working in his 80s, conducting and speaking to audiences about the Art of Possibility. He says, "Humans are addicted to possibility"[24]. Warren Buffet was still holding the reins at Berkshire Hathaway at the age of 92 (in 2023)[25]. And while Nobel Prizes are often awarded late in a person's career, the oldest recipient so far was Professor John B. Goodenough, who won the 2019 Nobel Prize for chemistry at 97 years old[26]. Jane Goodall, born in 1934, is still active, for instance lobbying the EU about caged farm animals[27]. Born in 1925, German native Johanna Quaas was the oldest active gymnast in the world[28], retiring in 2018. In 2020, when Sir David Attenborough was 93, he produced 'David Attenborough: A Life on Our Planet', in which he shared his thoughts on the future of the planet[29]. Finally, Yuichiro Miura is the oldest man ever to climb Everest, which he did aged 80[30].

[1] ilo.org – tinyurl.com/choices114
[2] Meadows, D., Randers, J., *Limits to Growth: The 30-Year Update,* Chelsea Green, 2004
[3] macrotrends.net – tinyurl.com/choices150
[4] reuters.com – tinyurl.com/choices115
[5] populationeducation.org – tinyurl.com/choices117
[6] Lustig, P. and Ringland, G., *Megatrends and How to Survive Them: preparing for 2032,* Cambridge Scholars Publishing, 2018
[7] ourworldindata.org – tinyurl.com/choices118
[8] ourworldindata.org – tinyurl.com/choices151
[9] axios.com – tinyurl.com/choices116
[10] who.int – tinyurl.com/choices119
[11] populationpyramid.net – tinyurl.com/choices469
[12] populationpyramid.net – tinyurl.com/choices470
[13] Cavendish, C., *Extra Time: 10 Lessons for an Ageing World,* HarperCollins, 2019
[14] 'Living to 120', *The Economist,* 30 September 2023
[15] who.int – tinyurl.com/choices120
[16] apps.who.int – tinyurl.com/choices351
[17] pop.org – tinyurl.com/choices501
[18] 'We need to talk about incels', *Financial Times Weekend,* 9 Sept. 2023
[19] unherd.com – tinyurl.com/choices466
[20] hrw.org – tinyurl.com/choices121
[21] *Empty Planet: the shock of global population decline,* Bricker, D. and Ibbotson, J., Robinson, 2019.
[22] icycanada.com – tinyurl.com/choices122
[23] bethecareconcept.com – tinyurl.com/choices124
[24] benjaminzander.org – tinyurl.com/choices502
[25] fool.com – tinyurl.com/choices125
[26] cockrell.utexas.edu – tinyurl.com/choices515
[27] education.nationalgeographic.org – tinyurl.com/choices465
[28] mymodernmet.com – tinyurl.com/choices468
[29] nytimes.com – tinyurl.com/choices126
[30] oldest.org – tinyurl.com/choices467

Chapter 9 – Urban Pull

- Most people live in urban areas, a major recent change.
- Women have fewer children when they live in urban areas.
- Productivity is higher in urban areas, increasing average incomes.

The story so far

Most people have better access to health, education and jobs when they move to urban areas. Already more than half the world's population lives in urban areas. When we speak of urban areas, we mean cities, market towns, informal settlements and even suburbs. We do not mean villages in rural areas. We use the terms 'city' and 'urban area' interchangeably.

People are moving from rural societies and economies to urban societies and their more developed economies. This is challenging many social structures. This migration will certainly continue beyond 2030[1]. Our story of urbanisation is a story about how effective cities involve local people and consider what people want of their city.

The graph **Migration to urban areas** shows its extent by region. Europe and North America had urbanised before 1950; the biggest changes since 1950 have been across the rest of the world.

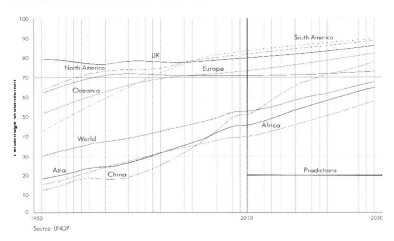

Figure 6: Migration to urban areas

In the developing economies of the Global Majority, with young, growing populations, densely populated cities and towns are expanding, typically through informal settlements with little or no infrastructure. About a quarter of the world's population live in informal settlements[2].

Mature cities with sprawling commuter patterns are also able to absorb new citizens.

Densely populated high-income cities like London, Hong Kong and New York are often the first stop for international immigrants. In mature economies with ageing and declining populations, the UN predicts that populations may still be continuing to grow in these larger urban areas until 2050.

Many small cities and towns are losing population[3] as the surrounding rural economy supports fewer people.

Most people moving to urban areas do so within their own country, for economic reasons. International migrants mostly move from poorer to richer countries. They help to support the economy in countries with declining populations as discussed in *Population*. They add to the workforce which, through taxation, helps to pay for social, health and public infrastructure.

In many ways, cities are good for people. There is much to be gained from proximity to others, especially for 'knowledge work'. Cities can be good for ethics[4]. Large metropolitan areas in mature economies can be up to 50% more productive and innovative than smaller ones[5]. In developing economies, the advantages of urban (and especially big city) living are even greater.

People migrate to urban areas to be near amenities. They can be closer to health care, entertainment and education. It is often easier to find work. As the UN Population Fund states in its 2007 report, "The best recipe for a life without poverty is to grow up in a city"[6].

As women move to urban areas and access education, the number of children they have tends to decrease. One of the best ways out of poverty is to live in a city[7]. Educating girls and women is especially effective because the benefits are felt throughout the community. An educated woman is better able to educate her own children and her children are more likely to attend school. The family is likely to be healthier and have a better income too.

Economic migrants to urban areas can, however, suffer from the lack of social support provided by extended family. And as rich and poor often live close to each other in cities, inequalities are apparent.

Other downsides of urban living include the higher cost of living, exposure to air pollution[8] (and the illness/mortality rates caused by this), commuting distances and times, and noise and light pollution. The Covid-19 pandemic is changing the conversation about how cities work, as more people use virtual working, they are commuting less. They use cities for leisure – data in *Mobility* illustrates this shift for London.

The design of cities is also a big factor in quality of life. Cities have a long lifetime – the built environment can last for centuries in both formal and informal settlements. So urban planning needs to consider not just how people want to live in cities now, but also how they might want to live in, and use, the urban space in several generations' time.

People living in formal cities today, live in cities designed by their grandparents' generation. The changes flagged in *Population* mean that families are now smaller than in their grandparents' time. People are now living longer. And as lifestyles are changing fast, this gives urban designers the challenge of anticipating how people's grandchildren will want to live in their cities.

If you want to explore what that might look like, think about a nearby city. How will you want to live in 20 years and what might a good life look like there, in that time? Think about the aspects of daily life and what is likely to be different and what will stay the same. Think about differences between what might reasonably be achieved in already built-up areas, in informal settlements and in newly built areas.

Informal settlements usually last longer than most people think they will. They require the same type of thinking – about how they will be used by people's grandchildren – as any other built environment, even if the buildings may be somewhat easier to demolish.

In new urban areas there are many possibilities and infrastructure can be designed to be fit for purpose. These new urban areas represent an amazing opportunity to design a smart city from scratch.

The massive shift in balance of population from rural to urban areas is challenging. Democracy is based on geography (people register to vote in a place) and many political structures still reflect the historic population map – when more people lived in rural areas than in cities. This means that rural areas and declining regions may have disproportionate political power today.

Cities and networks of cities are likely to claim a more influential role in the future. Economic migration has meant that London has more in common with New York City, Paris, Tokyo and Mumbai than it does with the rest of the UK. You might see something like one of the scenarios from *In Safe Hands*[9] which was called 'City States'. In this possible future, globalisation has failed. Democracy proved too unwieldy and Western value systems were judged to be inadequate. The idea of the nation state as provider and safety net has disappeared. Instead, up to 50 city states emerge, in some cases replacing a completely failed state. In other cases, the city state co-exists (occasionally awkwardly) with a national state whose role and authority are substantially reduced. Mobility between cities is the norm. The city states have very different strengths, weaknesses, wealth levels, regulatory regimes and brands.

The familiarity of cities perhaps makes it hard to realise what an amazing feat of human cooperation they are – 10 million people can't be kept in line by police or armies – cities depend on thousands of voluntary obligations between people without traditional family ties. This is perhaps the biggest shift from rural to urban life[10].

This Force for Change is the trend for people who have economic choices to move away from rural areas. A Threat that could deflect this trend temporarily is *Collapse of Global Health* for an extended time, for instance due to a pandemic.

Glimpses of Change

Urban resilience

- UNICITI (a network of urban planners who aim to revive and expand the uniqueness of Asian cities through sustainable and creative solutions[11]) has identified three elements of resilience that cities should aim to strengthen: public spaces, urban agriculture and quality of life[12].

- Freetown in Sierra Leone generates 30% of the country's GDP despite being home to only 15% of its population. The Transform Freetown initiative[13] was launched in 2019 with the aspiration for Freetown to emerge as a dynamic city of opportunity. The initiative has 11 priority sectors, grouped into four key clusters – Resilience, Human Development, Healthy City and Urban Mobility. Some targets include planting one million trees, scaling up digital literacy programmes, rolling out water kiosks and public toilets and developing five new street markets. The initiative is supported by collaboration and funding from many sources including the C40 Cities network[14].

Urban food security

- In Berlin, Germany, over 80,000 people have a vegetable garden and they grow fruit and vegetables in parks and on vacant plots. Tempelhof Airport now has 900 gardeners on 5,000 m² of land in a communal urban agriculture project. Another community project is the Prinzessinnengarten which reclaimed 6,000 m² of land after it had lain fallow for over 50 years[15].

Improving urban quality of life

- The Slum Networking project, initiated by engineer Himanshu Parikh in Indore, India sees informal settlements (slums) as an opportunity to introduce sustainable change to the city[16]. The project makes low-cost interventions like gravity-based sewers and storm drains, plants gardens and improves roads in slum areas. It has upgraded the area over 6 years with 90 km of new sewer pipes which increased the capacity of the main sewers, diverting sewage from the city's rivers and lakes, thus achieving better water quality for all in the city. New roads have reduced traffic congestion. Reclaiming degraded land for new green public space and upgraded infrastructure have improved life for all residents in the city.

15-minute Cities

- The C40 Coalition is an international coalition of urban leaders focused on fighting climate change and promoting sustainable development in cities. One recommendation was that all urban people should live in "15-minute cities" where they should be able to meet their shopping, work, education, healthcare, recreational and cultural needs all within a 15-minute walk or bicycle ride. It is the basis for most modern city designs. Most recently it has been articulated by Professor Carlos Moreno at the Sorbonne in Paris[17]. The mayor of Paris, Anne Hidalgo, pushed 'Paris Respire' to turn traffic lanes into cyclist friendly 'corona pistes', improving air quality and cutting down on unnecessary journeys[18]. Milan and Portland, Oregon are also moving in this direction[19].

[1] ourworldindata.org – tinyurl.com/choices504
[2] link.springer.com – tinyurl.com/choices354
[3] theconversation.com – tinyurl.com/choices152
[4] ethicalsystems.org – tinyurl.com/choices503
[5] papers.ssrn.com – tinyurl.com/choices153
[6] unfpa.org – tinyurl.com/choices353
[7] citymonitor.ai – tinyurl.com/choices348
[8] "Dirty old towns", *The Economist*, 19 August 2023
[9] zyen.com – tinyurl.com/choices154
[10] "A moral case for cities", *Financial Times*, 9 September 2023
[11] uniciti.org – tinyurl.com/choices516
[12] resilience.org – tinyurl.com/choices349
[13] fcc.gov.sl – tinyurl.com/choices471
[14] c40.org – tinyurl.com/choices472
[15] foodtank.com – tinyurl.com/choices344
[16] world-habitat.org – tinyurl.com/choices345
[17] nytimes.com – tinyurl.com/choices346
[18] france24.com – tinyurl.com/choices347
[19] nlc.org – tinyurl.com/choices350

Chapter 10 – Mobility

- People like to travel.
- Most forms of travel and transport are fossil fuel based.
- Both travel and transport are changing as the use of virtual connections increases.

The story so far

Ever since nomads travelled in search of pastures for their livestock and exchanged food, furs and animals, mobility and trade have been interlinked. As people travelled and traded, they shared stories of other places. This encouraged the wealthy to travel for the experiences. More recently, rising incomes and relatively cheap bicycles, cars and travel by ship or aeroplane have made it possible for more people than ever before to share the experience of travel to other places.

Meanwhile, mobility has been an essential enabler of economic activity and urbanisation. Over many decades, international trade has increased. There has been an expectation of continuing growth in traveling for pleasure, and transporting people and goods. So much so that the mode of travel is used as a key economic descriptor[1]. Applied to transport, at Level 1, people walk barefoot; at Level 2, the family has a bicycle and people have shoes; at Level 3, the family has a motorcycle and, at Level 4, people have a family car and many have been on an aeroplane.

Overall the cost of travel and transport is decreasing as more people travel and more goods are transported.

However we now wonder – will travel for pleasure continue to grow? Or are congestion at tourist locations, fear of disease, and options for virtual travel likely to limit physical travel for pleasure? How far are global supply chains being replaced by regional or local supply chains as international relations and the Backbones which support them fracture?

Urban transport

Since the world is increasingly urban, we start with urban transport.

The problems of congestion and air pollution in urban areas are expected to drive much of the innovation in urban people transport[2]. In densely populated fast-growing areas, often with informal settlements, shared transport is the norm. This includes buses, rail, metro systems, tuk-tuks, and water ferries.

Public transport is relatively advanced in the adoption of electric and hydrogen vehicles – for instance 100% of the buses in Shenzhen are electric[3]. Many areas are experimenting with hydrogen-fuelled buses. Urban rail is mostly electric; it is expected to double in passenger miles over the next 20 years and use mostly driverless trains.

In cities with sprawling commuter patterns, electric and hydrogen-fuelled private vehicles could become more widely used as they become cheaper, with longer range, shorter recharge times and a better charging infrastructure.

In densely populated high-income cities like London, Hong Kong and New York, demand for door-to-door transport could be met through e-scooters and e-bikes. The Covid-19 pandemic boosted cycling. Europeans are expected to buy an extra 10 million bicycles per year by 2030[4].

Within urban areas, freight distribution – particularly last-kilometre – is a major cause of congestion. Drones and e-vehicles may soon be the delivery vehicles of choice for small packages, while trucks are kept for bulky items. Skills shortages and cost pressures are already leading to the use of autonomous vehicles for freight transport by road[5].

Transport outside urban areas

For longer distances, between urban areas, the choices for travel and freight transport are changing.

Today road travel is the main form of transport for people and goods across most of the world. Much travel is by private car. So it is expected that the number of passenger cars will continue to grow: the International Energy Agency expects the number of passenger vehicles to increase by 600 million by 2035. Most of this increase is expected to be in China and other non-OECD countries[6].

China is investing heavily in railways with the Belt and Road Initiative (BRI) across Asia and Europe. The world's first 600 km/hour high speed maglev train has recently been launched in China[7]. It can fill the speed gap between high-speed rail, whose maximum operating speed is 350 km/h and aircraft, whose cruising speed is 800 to 900 km/h.

In many developing countries, air travel is preferable to travel on poor, slow roads. New ranges of smaller planes for up to 40 people, made of lighter materials and able to travel up to 10,000 km between smaller airports, are already eating into sales of extra-large aircraft[8].

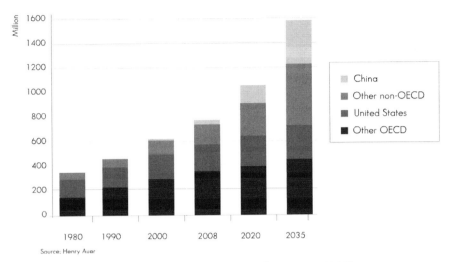

Figure 7: Passenger Vehicle numbers 1980-2035[9]

Estimates of the future of international air traffic vary widely, but it is expected to increase.[10] Drones are widely used in Africa to deliver drugs and other medical supplies in rural areas with poor road connectivity[11], as well as for a range of applications in agriculture – spraying and monitoring of crops. It does not include air taxis in cities – though these may well be a small niche market over the next decade[12].

The share of world trade which goes by sea has been reduced by competition from air, though it is still 80-90% of the total by volume and 60-70% by value[13]. Local manufacturing, as supply chains are rethought, and 3D printing expands, is likely to reduce air transport particularly of small, just-in-time items. There could also be a reduction in items shipped by sea in the longer term. The shipping industry – through the International Maritime Organisation – has plans to become net-zero by 2050[14]. Meanwhile, the BRI, recreating the old Silk Road from Asia to Europe, is expected to divert some freight traffic between Asia, Europe and Africa from sea routes to road and rail[15].

The role of Information and Communication Technology (ICT) in transport is increasing, both in management of infrastructure such as Smart Cities as discussed in *Connected World*, and through the transition to autonomous controls for freight, sea traffic, and trains. For instance in

Woolston, UK and Austin, Texas, Ocean Infinity[16] has remote operations centres that resemble a row of gamers playing but they are in fact remotely operating a fleet of supply and inspection ships.

Transitioning to fully autonomous vehicles for individual passengers (driverless cars) may be difficult[17]. The National Highway Traffic Safety Administration recognises levels[18]: at Level 1, Driver Assistance, individual controls such as cruise control are automated; at Level 2, Additional Driver Assistance, two or more may be automated, for instance adding lane control; at Level 3, Conditional Automation, the vehicle is in control, but the human is on standby; at Level 4, High Automation, the human may intervene, at Level 5, Full Automation, no controls are accessible to humans.

The difficulty is at Level 3, in which a vehicle reverts to human control on standby and the person has a split second to take over. Can they react in time? Who is in control?

No discussion of travel and transport would be complete without mentioning space travel. Space tourism flights are now offered to wealthy space tourists, initially at several hundred thousand dollars a ticket. And as the earth becomes denuded of key resources, the moon is an obvious target.

In August 2023, India's Chandrayaan-3 moon mission landed at the moon's south pole[19] and in February 2024, the Odysseus spacecraft also landed there[20]. The aim is to build a sustainable infrastructure for a Cislunar gateway (between the Earth and the Moon), lunar communications and bases, and develop mining of the lunar surface within the next decade. This could supply Helium-3 to fuel missions to Mars and beyond. By then, near space travel will be about transporting cargo and blue-collar workers[21].

The role of travel – particularly space travel and high-speed transport – in developing new technology is a topic in Peter Diamandis and Steven Kotler's *The Future is Faster than You Think*[22].

This Force for Change is a trend towards people travelling more for pleasure and less for work. The trend for increased global transport of goods may slow or reverse as *Fractured Backbones* limit the ability to agree common standards for information or components.

Glimpses of change

Transport as a Service

- Riversimple provides Transportation as a Service based on hydrogen-powered cars. Customers pay a monthly subscription for the car and all its associated running costs, including fuel. The current car, a "beautiful two seater, with a simple and spacious interior" is "the most energy efficient car on the planet". It does 0-55 miles per hour in 9 seconds, "is light to handle and fun to drive". It does about 250 miles per gallon and emits only water. Filling takes three minutes[23].

- Luxembourg: since 2020, all public transport modes, i.e. buses, trains and trams are free of charge everywhere[24].

New fuels

- The world's first hydrogen-electric passenger flight was successfully completed in September 2020. The six-seater ZeroAvia aircraft did a taxi, take-off, full pattern circuit and landing at an airfield in Cranfield, England[25]. Beyond Aero has plans for a business aircraft with a range of 800 miles, and Airbus made its first ever flight powered by a 100% hydrogen combustion engine in November 2023[26].
- Asia's huge motorcycle market is turning electric: in China, about half of two and three-wheel vehicles sold in 2021 were battery powered compared with 16% of cars[27].

Autonomous vehicles

- In Singapore, a shortage of truck drivers is being tackled with 'platoons' of four trucks with a single shared driver. This three-year pilot on public roads is designed to build up public trust[28].
- A fully autonomous ferry serves the islands south of Turku, Finland. The vessel uses sensors and AI to avoid collisions, and an autonomous navigation system for berthing. The captain is on land and can exercise remote control.

Virtual travel and transport

- Mercedes-Benz Trucks allows customers to 3D print a range of spare parts for freight trucks[29]. Siemens, a major rail equipment supplier, uses 3D printing for small-series custom train parts[30]. In 2021, the International Space Station's 3D printer manufactured the first 3D printed object in space, paving the way for future long-term space expeditions. The object, a print-head faceplate, is engraved with the names of the organisations that collaborated on this space station technology demonstration[31].

- Google Earth VR allows you to walk through Tokyo, fly over Yosemite or the Hoover Dam in the USA, climb the Matterhorn or explore Florence's cathedral[32]. You can also have a virtual tour of the Anne Frank House in Amsterdam[33]. Travel limitations during the Covid-19 pandemic have accelerated the introduction of virtual tours of galleries and historic buildings, of virtual gyms and house purchases without physical inspection of the property. Tour guides conduct groups around Barcelona, virtually[34]. Participants delight in the experience of the art and architecture, without the hassle of travel.
- The non-profit CyArk captures world heritage sites in 3D using LIDAR for posterity so that they can be used for education, virtual tourism and indeed should they become damaged by climate, natural disasters or acts of terrorism such as the destruction of the Bamiyan Buddhas in Afghanistan in 2000[35].

Changing lifestyles

Data from London Underground on daily passenger numbers in 2023 compared with 2019 describes a change in lifestyle in London from commuting to working from home and more leisure travel: daily ratios are approximately[36]:

- Sunday 130% - more passengers than in 2019
- Monday 75% - less passengers than in 2019
- Tuesday 90% - less
- Wednesday 85% - less
- Thursday 85% - less
- Friday 80% - less
- Saturday 115% - more

---

[1] Rosling, Hans, O. Rosling et al., *Factfulness: Ten Reasons We're Wrong about the World*, Sceptre, 2019

[2] etech.iec.ch – tinyurl.com/choices185

[3] mobilityforesights.com – tinyurl.com/choices474
[4] cyclingindustries.com – tinyurl.com/choices190
[5] porttechnology.org – tinyurl.com/choices191
[6] iea.org – tinyurl.com/choices192
[7] chinatravel.com – tinyurl.com/choices475
[8] "Flying taxis take off", The Economist. 18 August 2023
[9] https://warmgloblog.blogspot.com/search?q=passenger+vehicle+numbers
[10] iata.org – tinyurl.com/choices193
[11] nation.africa – tinyurl.com/choices188
[12] ft.com – tinyurl.com/choices342
[13] unctad.org – tinyurl.com/choices186
[14] theconversation.com – tinyurl.com/choices189
[15] tandfonline.com – tinyurl.com/choices343
[16] https://oceaninfinity.com
[17] See AI Chapter for autonomous taxis
[18] thewindscreenco.co.uk – tinyurl.com/choices194
[19] "India's historic moon mission", *New Scientist*, 2 September 2023.
[20] space.com – tinyurl.com/choices356
[21] spaceforcejournal.org – tinyurl.com/choices505
[22] Diamandis, P. and Kotler, S. *The Future is Faster than You Think*, Simon & Schuster, 2020.
[23] www.riversimple.com
[24] luxembourg.public.lu – tinyurl.com/choices473
[25] https://zeroavia.com/
[26] hydrogeninsight.com – tinyurl.com/choices184
[27] "Swap Teams", *The Economist*, 16th September 2023
[28] As reference 4
[29] 3dprintingindustry.com – tinyurl.com/choices187
[30] mobility.siemens.com – tinyurl.com/choices195
[31] nasa.gov – tinyurl.com/choices355
[32] vrlowdown.com – tinyurl.com/choices183
[33] annefrank.org – tinyurl.com/choices196
[34] thegeographicalcure.com – tinyurl.com/choices341
[35] https://www.cyark.org/
[36] "Department for Transport", *Financial Times Datawatch*, 9th August 2023

Chapter 11 – Energy Choices

- The world economy is still dependent on fossil fuels but it is changing fast to renewables.
- This is going to be a very severe, disruptive change with questions about who pays.
- Electricity is the new oil and it is already a much cheaper energy source.

The story so far

The twentieth century was the century of fossil fuel. It was used for generating electricity, for heating, for powering the engines used for everything from manufacturing to travel and transport, and as the basic ingredient for materials such as plastics and petrochemicals. The price of a barrel of oil was a key economic factor.

Concern over global heating from CO_2 emissions is behind the move away from the use of fossil fuels to generate electricity or to power engines. Electricity is now increasingly generated without burning fossil fuels – using hydro, nuclear, wind and solar.

The twenty-first century will be the century of electricity and renewable energy. Today, society depends on electricity to light our buildings, power our electronic equipment and increasingly – as more vehicles become electric – to run our transport systems. In the Global North – and in the Majority World as their economies mature – electricity is expected to be available 24/7. A key metric is now becoming the price of a kWh of electricity. This is likely to push the transition to renewables since they are cheaper per kWh than fossil fuels for electricity generation.

How quickly the transition from fossil fuels to renewables will happen depends on the choices that people and national governments make. These choices will depend on the trade-offs: influenced by carbon emissions, technology, costs, infrastructure and international relations. However, there is evidence that emissions from electricity generated by fossil fuels may have peaked as growth in demand is increasingly met by renewables[1].

Russia's invasion of Ukraine changed fossil fuel use, as sanctions drove prices higher, fossil fuel companies reaped previously unexpected rewards[2].

European countries, caught out by their reliance on Russian gas, worked hard to reduce their dependence and shifted away from Russian imports and towards both greater renewable energy and new LNG (Liquified Natural Gas) contracts, closing down much existing supply from Russian pipelines[3]. New regassification facilities were relatively quickly built to diversify overall fossil fuel supply and accommodate the new LNG supplies.

The carbon emissions created in generating energy vary widely according to the fuel: very high for coal and wood and low for renewables and nuclear. Electricity generation from natural gas has grown significantly over the last two decades – this is the only fossil fuel that is likely to continue to increase its use, as it is the least 'bad' of the fossil fuels, with the lowest emissions.

The Carbon Footprint think tank compiles data on CO_2 emissions per kWh for many countries – the figure below compares some countries, from their August 2018 report[4]. We were fascinated to see the big differences in countries with similar economies – for instance, France and Germany. France gets nearly three quarters of its energy from nuclear power: in most countries it is a smaller part of the mix.

The EU, UK, Japan and China, among others, have declared zero emission timescales, largely due to social pressure. A nation's choices about the mix of energy sources will involve a trade-off between the options, and making the best choices with regards to the environment (global warming and pollution), the economy and cost to consumers.

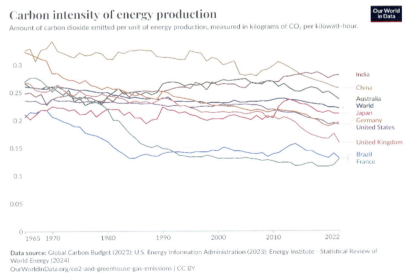

Figure 8: CO_2 emitted per kWh generated[5]

Overall, the motivation for the move from fossil fuels may well be economic. The International Energy Agency notes that "The world's best solar power schemes now offer the 'cheapest ... electricity in history' with the technology cheaper than coal and gas in most major countries"[6].

Fossil fuels will still be an important part of the energy mix for years because of the existing infrastructure (renewables require new distribution infrastructure), the lack of suitable replacement fuel for applications like aviation[7], and the manufacture of steel and concrete[8].

A new business model

The business model for energy infrastructure has been a centralised (national) grid which distributes electricity produced by large generating plants. Fluctuations in electricity usage (peak times) are handled by capacity lying idle and ready to go on-line as demand arises.

In terms of distribution, hydro-electricity and nuclear fit this pattern, whilst solar and wind do not. Utility companies are being challenged because sources of renewable electricity are not in the same places as fossil fuel powered electricity generation plants, and new technologies are needed for storage to handle intermittency and demand spikes. As the demand for electricity goes up, infrastructure is increasingly being challenged. *The Washington Post* makes the challenge clear: "Vast swaths of the United States are at risk of running short of power as electricity-hungry data centers and clean-technology factories proliferate around the country, leaving utilities and regulators grasping for credible plans to expand the nation's creaking power grid."[9]

Energy from solar or wind is intermittent in many areas – it isn't always sunny or windy. This energy needs to be stored when it is abundant, so that it can be used at times when it isn't. This means more trade-offs – what is available? what does it cost to produce the energy in both money and emissions? how is it to be stored and transferred? For instance, in areas like Sub-Saharan Africa, distribution problems mean that there are countries where less than half of the population has access to electricity from the grid[10]. Here micro grids based on solar energy are being developed to reach people who otherwise would be without electricity.

Space-based solar power collects energy from the sun using panels on satellites and beams it safely back to Earth. The UK has established the Space Energy Initiative to develop Space-Based Solar Power, while the European

Commission is funding a project investigating large lightweight reflectors redirecting sunlight onto solar farms on the ground called SOLARIS[11].

New technology, infrastructure and networks are not yet able to fully support a shift to solar and wind power when there are intermittency problems. One fast developing area to cover this is the technology for electricity storage. For example, there are a few new sites available for pumped hydro. Water is pumped to the higher reservoir and can be released to the lower reservoir to collect the hydro energy when needed. Stored 'green' hydrogen – sometimes mixed with natural gas – is also being explored for seasonal storage[12].

Batteries or fuel cells for storage of course also have a carbon footprint from their manufacture. Currently, lithium-ion batteries are the most popular alternative to traditional lead-acid batteries, due to their longevity and energy density.

While there is progress on battery development, there isn't yet a perfect electricity storage method available.

There is much written about hydrogen as a renewable. It is beginning to be part of the energy mix. Making hydrogen can be a very dirty and energy intensive process. It can also be clean (called green hydrogen) when it is made using renewable energy, and is thought to be able to play a major role in global emissions reduction after 2030[13]. Hydrogen made from excess energy from wind or solar can be stored for later use[14]. Existing gas pipeline networks can be gradually converted to hydrogen operation with an investment of an estimated 10-15% of the cost of new construction using existing technologies[15]. Hydrogen can be used to heat buildings and it can be used to power vehicles.

Nuclear power is an increasing part of the mix in China, India, Russia, and South Korea, with new plants under construction. But it may not contribute much to the mix of energy sources in other countries that are planning to phase it out as ageing plants approach the end of their life. The development of small modular reactors (SMRs), advanced nuclear reactors that have a power capacity of up to 300 MW(e) per unit, which is about one-third of the generating capacity of traditional nuclear power reactors, is offering new options for rural and remote areas[16, 17].

Over the next decades, changes in the energy mix used in shipping are expected to lead to cleaner shipping with more efficient engines, possibly using ammonia batteries, hydrogen fuel cells, or small nuclear reactors.

Heating of buildings is a major energy use. Currently gas and oil boilers and furnaces are the predominant source: heat pumps are proposed as the best alternative. These extract ambient heat from the outside air, even when it is below freezing, and concentrate it to warm inside spaces[18]. However, their introduction into domestic markets is proving difficult for many reasons[19].

Coal-powered plants are being taken out of service in OECD countries, and China and India are slowing the growth of new coal-powered electricity generation. However, both China and India continue to build new installations and many of their coal-powered plants are still less than 15 years old.

While there are enough of the key minerals that the world will need for the transition to renewables, it will be a challenge to increase supply fast enough to meet demand in the short term[20] for the minerals now needed for batteries[21].

New battery designs have reduced future cobalt needs[22] – nickel-free Lithium Iron Phosphate (LFP) batteries are replacing them and lithium can be recycled to make new batteries[23]. Many of the Chinese battery makers that dominate the market are working on semi-solid versions which would double the range of EVs and extend the range of small air taxis. Sodium-ion batteries are also proposed, made from agricultural waste[24], for applications which need better safety characteristics than lithium. Possible battery alternatives are also sought in water, gold and ammonia[25].

There could be a shift in power and influence from oil producing regions to those that produce lithium and the components needed for EVs, batteries and renewable power generation.

The choices the world makes about its energy mix are going to be fascinating to watch; we suspect there will be surprises in store.

This Force for Change is the trend away from fossil fuels. Threats that could affect this trend are *Global Heating*, as extreme weather events cause organisations and governments to speed up plans to decarbonise; and *Fractured Backbones* which could delay the trend away from fossil fuels.

Glimpses of change

Solar power

- M-KOPA, based in Kenya and pan-African, is putting SIM cards into solar lights. Since they can be tracked, it is viable to lease the lights for 50 cents a day, instead of buying them. This decreases kerosene costs and reduces health impacts of using wood to create

light, it raises exam pass rates and gives access to finance and insurance[26].
- India's National Thermal Power Corporation (NTPC) is developing floating solar plants, where the photovoltaic panels are deployed on the surface of water. NTPC officials explain that setting up floating solar units on places like reservoirs helps in cutting down on the costs, as South India has a large number of major reservoirs. As five acres of land is required to set up a 1 MW solar photo-voltaic plant and given the challenges in land acquisitions, they are going for floating plants[27].

Wind power

- Wind power has a history in Canada dating back many decades, particularly on prairie farms. As of December 2019, wind power generating capacity provided about 6% of Canada's electricity demand. The Canadian Wind Energy Association has outlined a future strategy for wind energy that would reach a capacity of 55 GW by 2025, meeting 20% of the country's energy needs[28].
- Laura Watts' *Energy at the End of the World: An Orkney Islands Saga* tells how Orkney now has 700 micro-wind turbines which are household, local-owned turbines about the size of a farmhouse, along with six large-scale, island-owned wind turbines. The islands are also the world's centre for tidal energy research, and they have had a smart grid for ten years. Orkney islanders generate 120% of their energy needs[29].

Rethinking sources of energy

- Ammonia is being considered as a fuel for shipping. The advantage of ammonia is that it liquefies at -33°C compared with -253°C for hydrogen. The energy density is much higher in ammonia than in hydrogen, so that ammonia can be both an energy carrier and fuel in itself, replacing hydrogen. Equinor has announced that it is aiming to have a vessel running on ammonia in test operations in 2024[30].

---

[1] "Emissions from renewables may have peaked", *New Scientist,* 22 April 2023
[2] weforum.org – tinyurl.com/choices203

[3] reuters.com – tinyurl.com/choices204
[4] ourworldindata.org – tinyurl.com/choices506
[5] ourworldindata.org – tinyurl.com/choices197
[6] carbonbrief.org – tinyurl.com/choices205
[7] royalsociety.org – tinyurl.com/choices478
[8] nature.com – tinyurl.com/choices359
[9] washingtonpost.com – tinyurl.com/choices198
[10] statista.com – tinyurl.com/choices206
[11] esa.int – tinyurl.com/choices199
[12] sserenewables.com – tinyurl.com/choices207
[13] rmi.org – tinyurl.com/choices517
[14] theguardian.com – tinyurl.com/choices208
[15] assets.siemens-energy.com – tinyurl.com/choices335
[16] iaea.org – tinyurl.com/choices476
[17] Russia's Akademik Lomonosov, the world's first floating nuclear power plant that began commercial operation in May 2020, is producing energy from two 35 MW(e) SMRs.
[18] "Heat pumps in hot water", *The Economist*, 9 September 2023
[19] building.co.uk – tinyurl.com/choices336
[20] "Myths are clouding the reality of our sustainable energy future" by Adair Turner, *Financial Times*, 20.07.2023.
[21] "The new commodity superpowers" by Leslie Hook, Harry Dempsy and Ciara Nugent, *Financial Times*, 09.08.2023.
[22] ft.com – tinyurl.com/choices358
[23] as note 3
[24] pubs.acs.org – tinyurl.com/choices477
[25] euronews.com – tinyurl.com/choices334
[26] ft.com – tinyurl.com/choices362
[27] energy.economictimes.indiatimes.com – tinyurl.com/choices200
[28] statista.com – tinyurl.com/choices202
[29] Watts, L. *Energy at the End of the World: An Orkney Islands Saga*, MIT Press, 2018
[30] marinelink.com – tinyurl.com/choices357

Chapter 12 – Connected World

- The Connected World is now widespread.
- This means that availability and resilience of networks is important to societies and economies.
- The economic and social impacts of a Connected World are yet to be fully understood.

The story so far

Most people can now access digital services for commerce, entertainment and information; and sensor devices are controlling networks across the globe. The *Connected World* can be a lever to achieve positive changes for people. Social changes brought about through the *Connected World* can be disruptive and result in calls for improved regulation. This is masking some of the positives.

It is about 60 years since computers started to automate governments and firms and about 35 years since personal computers and the first web browser made the internet accessible. We will discuss in *Economic Activity* how ICT[1] has now become pervasive in everyday life.

In 2022, 63% of the global population used the internet[2]. In 2024 there were estimated to be nearly 5 billion people using smartphones[3]. A lower estimate of the number of sensors connected to the internet is 50 billion in 2023[4], with wide expectations of continuing growth.

Applications (apps) are the visible bits of the connected world. Apps use a world-wide infrastructure of wireless and hard-wired networks, software and data. Apps run on increasing numbers and types of devices such as sensors and drones, as well as the familiar smartphones, PCs, play stations and cameras. Apps run social media, supply chain systems, workflow software and personnel scheduling packages. They provide platforms, for instance, replacing estate agents with search engines and data, or deskilling part of the work of lawyers and accountants.

The growth of the use and complexity of IT platforms is a major destabilising factor. We explore some of the effects on the economy in *Economic Activity* and on society in *Social Change*.

In this chapter we use four domains to illustrate the way in which the connected world is a lever for change – financial services; infrastructure and smart cities; entertainment and social media; and digital systems. We do not have space to describe the many other uses – from agriculture, online shopping, travel, and education to healthcare. All present a similar range of challenges for governments and organisations to ensure that their use is beneficial to users, such as the disruptive effect of application platforms on the economy and society.

Financial services

Financial services – banking, trading, investing, and insurance – were among the earliest users of ICT. Mobile technology and low cost, easy-to-use platforms have revolutionised access to finance for consumers via phones, cameras and computers. Systems such as Wise transfer money efficiently for a low fee and a good rate of exchange. Beggars and buskers in China are using QR (electronically readable) codes to accept donations. A recent G4S report[5] concluded: "China is getting rid of all cash and is quickly becoming a cashless society." The use of cash reduced further during the Covid-19 pandemic.

Banks' business of transferring payments is being challenged by trading platforms based on blockchain software. A blockchain is a computer program providing a shared, unchangeable distributed ledger that is transparent, highly secure, and viewable only by those on a permitted network: unlike a traditional trading platform there is no central hub. Blockchain is the technology that enables the existence of cryptocurrencies (among other things). Although we can't see or touch cryptocurrencies, they do hold value. Cryptocurrencies can be stored in a digital wallet on a smartphone or computer, and owners can use them to purchase things[6]. This is clearly not subject to the same control from governments as flows of currency across national boundaries.

Bitcoin is the best-known cryptocurrency. In 2016, Canada was accepting bitcoin when I (Patricia) had to pay for a work permit. However, at the time of writing the valuation of cryptocurrencies and their market is very volatile, spooking many potential users. The market is dominated by the top 20 crypto currencies which account for nearly 90% of the total market[7] and the top 100 have published – albeit changing – dollar equivalences.

Infrastructure and smart cities

Smart cities use digital infrastructure: many projects were originally proposed to give online access to government services and to underpin a high level of citizen participation. "One key goal was to develop the Open City

Toolkit (OCT), a collection of tools, software, libraries and apps that can empower citizens to participate in and shape the future of their cities," says Christian Kray, scientific coordinator, head of the Situated Computing and Interaction Lab at the University of Münster, Germany. "The toolkit would help to deliver services based on open data that are useful for citizens, businesses and governing bodies alike."[8] The term 'safe city' mainly describes the automation of policing using video cameras. The *Financial Times* Big Read in June 2021[9] stated that "The security risks of smart cities" also covered "safe cities". The technology and systems to implement both are dominated by Chinese technology suppliers. For instance Chinese firm Huawei's cloud infrastructure and e-government services handle citizens' data on tax, health and legal records in 41 countries[10]. The methodology for implementing a smart city is described in Tan Zhanglu's *Smart Cities*[11]. At the same time, governments and citizens are beginning to be alarmed at the potential for misuse of the technologies used in safe city software, like facial recognition. We will come back to this in *AI*.

However, smart cities today face the challenge of making sure that their policies and regulation keep up with the technology. "'Cities are continuing to invest heavily in new technologies to automate and improve city services and urban life. Yet our findings validate our fears that most cities are falling behind when it comes to ensuring effective oversight and governance of these technologies", said Jeff Merritt, Head of Internet of Things and Urban Transformation, World Economic Forum.[12]

Entertainment

Digital entertainment has seen major growth with over 2.5 billion gamers around the world. The industry demonstrates the potential and also the problems of the connected world: security is the biggest challenge to the industry. Data breaches in 2020 resulted in over 10 billion cyber-attacks using stolen lists of usernames and passwords[13]. And that doesn't include Distributed Denial of Services (DDoS) attacks, where a site is flooded with traffic; spoofing emails from sites with names intended to be mistaken for trusted sites, etc.

Social media

Finally, social media is a source of much enjoyment to many people, enabling them to connect virtually at any time and in (almost) any place. It is pervasive and embedded. The Covid-19 pandemic extended its reach. It has changed people's ideas about what can be achieved without physical visits or physical transfers of money and goods. However there is worrying data which suggests that teenage mental health problems rise with use of social media[14]; and the rise of social media has changed the way that democracy works[15] – with results thought to be positive in many regions, though negative in the USA. Pew Research Center, in an article from December 2022, says that "majorities in most of the 19 nations surveyed believe social media has been a good thing for democracy in their country. Assessments are especially positive in Singapore, Malaysia, Poland, Sweden, Hungary and Israel, where 65% or more hold this view". They felt that social media made them less powerless because it informed them and raised public awareness. However, even those who saw social media in a positive light regarding democracy admitted that it had led to manipulation and division in societies.

It is possible to argue that regulation always lags behind innovation, and innovation is adopted by criminals before the police, but that systems catch up[16] – current examples are online fraud and banking scams. Sometimes, however, it is hard to stay calm when technological capability is used to the detriment of society.

Digital systems

All systems are dependent on the data they use. Much data held by organisations contains factual errors of one sort or another and as the saying goes, 'garbage in, garbage out'. Errors are often left for to the consumer to correct. Jim Balsillie, former chief executive of Research in Motion, has proposed a first step in regulating the use and valuation of data[17]. He suggests that the International Monetary Fund should help coordinate global data rules for a joint international strategy for dealing with the impact of technology. "In 1976, 16% of the value of the S&P [index] was intangibles [but] today intangibles comprise almost 90% of the S&P's total value." It has become an issue recognised by The World Economic Forum which has proposed the concept of a data bank account[18]. A person's data, it suggests, should "…reside in an account where it would be controlled, managed, exchanged and accounted for."

Digital systems are also dependent on the underpinning networks. Recently, concern is being expressed that 99% of internet traffic travels through undersea cables[19] – with obvious opportunity for sabotage. Digital systems are also dependent on the software that implements the algorithms[20] and in the UK alone it is estimated that software failures cost the economy more than road accidents.

The world is increasingly dependent on ICT systems, and the demands on energy supply are rising. Currently the projections are that demand from data centres and fixed (telecoms) networks could almost double through to 2030 from the 2025 total of 5% to 9%[21].

Platforms are evolving over many domains to change the balance of power. They increase the skill needed by the few who design the platform and reduce the skill of the many who operate the systems.

The platforms increasingly dominating the supply of digital services have monopolistic characteristics[22] – from Amazon to Apple. Consumers benefit in the short term but in the USA, President Biden issued an executive order which calls on the Federal Trade Commission to craft new rules on Big Tech's data collection and user surveillance practices, and asks the agency to prohibit certain unfair methods of competition in internet marketplaces[23].

In summary, across many aspects of the *Connected World*, the pace of change means that societal understanding and regulatory regimes have not yet emerged to ensure the positives outweigh the negatives.

This Force for Change is for increasing dependence of both society and the economy on a *Connected World*. This could be disrupted by the lack of coherence arising from *Fractured Backbones*. One effect of *Global Heating* could be pressure to reduce travel and transport, with their impact on carbon emissions, and to increase the use of virtual connections for business and leisure.

Glimpses of Change

Financial services

- In Africa, M-Pesa has revolutionised access to finance using mobile phones. It allows users to store money on their phones. If you want to pay a bill, or send money to a friend, you text it and the recipient can convert it into cash at their local M-Pesa office. It means that millions of Africans who do not have a bank account can still manage their finances[24].
- Cryptocurrency in developing nations can help tackle corruption through a transparent structure. "We might see more developing countries implementing regulations or laws to promote innovation and digitalisation. Developing countries, such as India, can use cryptocurrencies to combat corruption by providing transparency and immutability to financial transactions."[25]

Infrastructure – smart cities

- In advising a regional government on what could help recovery after the Covid-19 pandemic, I (Gill) focused on a robust IT infrastructure. Equally important are the skills to be able to effectively use IT applications in health care, agriculture and the home. This means understanding data security, systems recovery and resilience. Supporting end users without these skills is important too, as the patchy effect of home schooling has shown.
- The positive effect of the connected world in enabling human connections is not often celebrated. So it was good to hear Richard Benyon, long time UK MP, say in a [Zoom] Forum, "My time as an MP could have been so much more productive if I had this sort of session, made possible through the new technology, early on in my tenure."[26]

Entertainment

- The online game Fortnite held a championship in 2019. The duo that won was a team of two boys: Aqua (aka David Wang) from Austria and Nyhrox (aka Emil Bergquist Pedersen) from Norway. They won despite being the underdogs and living in different countries so that they had never met face to face[27].

Social media

- Millennials used social media to respond after the 2015 Nepal earthquakes. In the face of slow government help reaching remote areas, the Yellow House in Sanepa emerged as a hub of "vibrant guerrilla aid". A team run by a handful of young Millennials armed with Facebook, open source mapping technology and local knowledge put out a call on Facebook to "see what we can do". Hundreds of people came to help. People in Belgium and the USA raised funds, others helped to develop online maps for local volunteers to deliver aid to some of the quake's hardest-hit areas. The UN saw what they were doing and supplied rice, tarpaulins and equipment – supporting an effort that was effective [28].
- See the *Glimpse of Change* on p. 43 on the Collaborate 2020 conference.

[1] Was Information and Communications Technology: now more generally the infrastructure and components that underpin digital systems.
[2] data.worldbank.org – tinyurl.com/choices507
[3] bankmycell.com – tinyurl.com/choices479
[4] statista.com – tinyurl.com/choices161
[5] ft.com – tinyurl.com/choices329
[6] bbc.co.uk – tinyurl.com/choices518
[7] statista.com – tinyurl.com/choices365
[8] ec.europa.eu – tinyurl.com/choices156
[9] Exporting Chinese surveillance: the security risks of 'smart cities' | Financial Times (ft.com) – tinyurl.com/choices363
[10] Huawei's Global Cloud Strategy (csis.org) – tinyurl.com/choices332
[11] Zhanglu, T. and Jing, X. *Smart Cities: Framework and Practice*, Royal Collins Publishing Company 2020
[12] weforum.org – tinyurl.com/choices333
[13] akamai.com – tinyurl.com/choices155
[14] bbc.co.uk – tinyurl.com/choices480
[15] pewresearch.org – inyurl.com/choices160
[16] ft.com – tinyurl.com/choices330
[17] hub.packtpub.com – tinyurl.com/choices164
[18] www3.weforum.org – tinyurl.com/choices158
[19] ingenia.org.uk – tinyurl.com/choices157
[20] bcs.org – tinyurl.com/choices364
[21] enerdata.net – tinyurl.com/choices162
[22] knowledge.insead.edu – tinyurl.com/choices167
[23] cnbc.com – tinyurl.com/choices159
[24] Driven by purpose: 15 years of M-Pesa's evolution | McKinsey – tinyurl.com/choices331
[25] financialexpress.com – tinyurl.com/choices163
[26] Personal conversation
[27] edition.cnn.com – tinyurl.com/choices166
[28] unhcr.org – tinyurl.com/choices165

Chapter 13 – AI

- AI already outperforms humans in a range of white-collar and blue-collar applications and board games.
- AI's weaknesses include reinforcing existing biases and potentially making false decisions and assertions which may not be evident as false and are difficult to check.
- Regulation of AI lags behind its adoption.

The story so far

AI (Artificial Intelligence) is often hailed as the new oil – with promises of replacing human intelligence. AI has become a focus of international competition between the US and China[1], although any productivity revolution is likely to be a decade away[2].

'Superintelligence', when AI systems can replicate or surpass the complete range of human capabilities, is not here today. Timescale estimates cluster around 2040[3], but nobody knows whether it is achievable at all because there isn't yet enough data to go on. Superintelligence raises existential issues[4], but we think that, with effective regulation, the risks can likely be mitigated.

The story so far has been dominated by machine learning (ML): historic data is used to train software algorithms to make decisions, control robots or drones, etc. Artificial General Intelligence (AGI) systems, unlike most current systems, would be smarter than the best human experts, and train themselves to become better over time. This has been achieved in specific domains, such as the game of Go[5].

AI to augment humans

One of the challenges raised by AI capabilities is how work might be modified or redesigned to use AI in a complementary rather than substitution role. The sciences and medicine have been early to adopt AI technology for analysing data. In geological applications like mining and exploration, computer vision and AI are used together to interpret data archived over the years[6].

There seem to be two approaches which are revolutionising science[7]: literature-based discovery to look for connections, and robot scientists to formulate and test hypotheses, leading to dramatically faster discovery of new drugs[8].

AI has been crucial in the hunt for vaccines[9], new proteins[10] and antibiotics[11] by interpreting and synthesising data. It is also used to look for correlations between drugs and symptoms and for diagnosis[12].

Patient recovery rates improve under robotic surgery, using very small tools attached to a robotic arm[13].

Two social forces are driving Chinese AI development[14]: the demand for services from consumers in dense urban settlements, and the challenge of providing access to affordable and high-quality services for its ageing population. China is looking to combine AI with medical and biometric data to provide personalised healthcare to more people at a lower cost, while keeping them healthier through continuous monitoring and alerts. Other applications of AI are to assist medical professionals in decision making, track patient outcomes, reduce physician workload and speed up drug development. These developments could spread to developing countries in the Majority World.

Manufacturing has used robots for many years, with Japan originally leading in their use. Figure 9 shows the density of robots in industry, across a range of countries. In 2021 South Korea had the highest proportion of robots in the manufacturing workforce at about 10% and China had a higher density of robot use than the USA[15].

Many management and customer service jobs have already been partially automated by AI systems. But AI is not only affecting white-collar jobs. It also supports and replaces jobs ranging from truck driving to manufacturing, to labour-intensive front-line services such as cleaning and nursing, to agriculture, to dangerous occupations and the military. AI is embedded in robots, drones and other devices. In social care, pet robots are also already in wide use to provide company, able to respond to touch and voice. Other robots do dangerous jobs such as firefighting and tackling contaminated sites[16], underwater work, exploration and production of oil, gas and minerals, and crime fighting. Infantry is the single biggest user of manpower in the military, so China and the USA are developing robots to work alongside human infantry. Meanwhile the war being fought in

Robot Density: manufacturing industry top 12, 2022

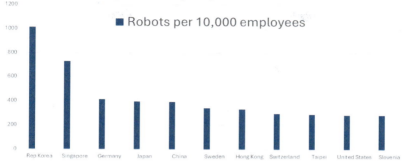

Ukraine is combining all of it – drones, robots, AI, targeting through phone locations, etc.

Figure 9: The Countries with the Highest Density of Robot Workers[17]

The use of AI is expected to continue and develop. So the number of jobs done by humans and the skills that humans need in the future are expected to be different from today.

'The Future of Skills'[18] report found that around 10% of the workforce are in occupations that are likely to grow as a share of the workforce: education, healthcare and wider public sector occupations. Around 20% are in occupations that are likely to shrink. Skills that are likely to be in greater demand in the future include: interpersonal, higher-order cognitive, systems thinking and integrative thinking. Estimates are that two thirds of today's schoolchildren could be employed eventually in jobs that have yet to be created[19].

Validation and verification of AI systems

As AI moves beyond augmenting humans and as AI systems start to replace humans, it becomes important to understand the basis of decisions made by AI systems. Decisions made by AI systems use software algorithms developed by their designers, and are trained by data chosen to be relevant. Both data choices and algorithms are recognised to have biases.

The quality and quantity of data to train AI systems has been a limiting factor in their application. In the world of recruitment, the use of AI is found to penalise women as the data has been built up historically[20] and reflects the bias embedded in past practice. And the sheer volume of data needed to build large language models (LLMs) such as ChatGPT is stunning. It was trained on 570 gigabytes of text data, or about 300 billion words – more than the total number of words in the collection of the British Library[21]. These models will increasingly be built on data generated by LLMs and hence degrade in quality[22].

Bias in legal, medical and recruitment decisions made by humans is well known. This can result from assumptions arising from a person's name, appearance, or voice. Additionally, human decisions are affected by 'noise'[23] – factors such as a good lunch! So in comparing AI decisions with human decisions, we may be comparing the imperfect decisions made with one (AI) set of biases with the imperfect decisions made by humans with another set of biases plus some very human factors.

An important life skill is the ability to judge the veracity of data. Apps can judge the likelihood of images being AI-generated and hence fake[24]; and students' essays are checked for ChatGPT characteristics[25]. Finland has had media literacy education, starting in kindergarten and continuing through basic education and adult education, since the 1970s, and believes it helps to mitigate information pollution[26].

However, there is concern that AI systems are increasingly being used in circumstances where there is no practical way to query or compare the outcomes[27]; for instance in the evaluation of CVs as part of a selection or recruitment process, as criteria for getting credit or a mortgage, and in court sentences. One suggestion is that AI could be part of a company's board of directors by 2026 [28].

A recent exercise by the author (Gill) asked ChatGPT "what are the 3 major software risks?" The answer came back citing an article that does not exist, in a journal that does exist, by an academic who does exist, so it is hard to recognise the information as false except by searching journal archives or contacting the named author[29]. Academics are finding that they need to check that the references in academic articles are not fake[30].

Machine learning algorithms used today in healthcare, education and criminal justice are making judgements which reflect the cultural biases of the designers of those systems: of the nine major platforms incorporating AI, six are based in the USA and three are in China; and designers and implementers are mostly male, young and college educated[31]. The cultural biases of designers are also important. For instance, an MIT survey of drivers asked them to make choices involving loss of life. Participants from China, Japan and South Korea were more likely to spare the lives of the elderly: those from USA, Canada and France were more inclined to spare young people[32]. Will your autonomous car include an algorithm to save young people or the elderly? How would you know?

The algorithms learn from the corpus of data collected. This data reflects the biases of the society which created it. So for example such systems may build in lower salaries for women, based on history[33], or make racist decisions based on names or facial characteristics[34].

Generative AI describes algorithms (such as ChatGPT) that can be used to create new content, including audio, software code, images, text, simulations, and videos. This is more disruptive than the augmentation of jobs by AI systems; Hollywood script writers went on strike over the use of AI written scripts[35].

AI, regulation and ethics

AI is used extensively by organisations to influence people to buy products, services, and political ideas. Currently, the burden is on the individual to judge what they are being told. The view is emerging that this should change: the onus should be on organisations to provide transparency of data sources and algorithms. This is also relevant for 'fake news' when doctored, or totally fake photos, speech or videos are used in political campaigns.

Agreement on the ethics of the use of all AI technologies lags behind their adoption, with regulation even further behind. There is international focus on the need for regulation of AI[36] but approaches differ. The US federal government's approach to AI risk management can broadly be characterised as risk-based, sectorally specific, and highly distributed across federal agencies[37]. The EU's recent guidelines[38] are based on the idea that AI should respect rights and be robust enough to avoid unintentional harm.

AI is being used both positively – for instance in science-based discovery; and negatively in its extensive use in warfare, where AI is embedded in drones and weapons; and in targeted disinformation. This could be disrupted by increasing conflict in *International Relations*, pushing further development of drones as weapons. Effective regulation could stall due to the lack of coherence arising from *Fractured Backbones*.

AI is often seen as an existential risk. However the long-term AI risk is largely unknowable. When people have a clear idea of the risk, they can develop concrete steps for mitigation. With AI, the difficulty of envisioning what the long-term risk could be means that it may not be possible to develop concrete steps to reduce it. It may then be better to focus on the shorter-term risks that can be more clearly identified.

Glimpses of Change

AI to augment humans

- A contest to find loopholes fastest was organised in the US between five experienced lawyers and an AI trained to read contracts[39]. The AI found 94% of the loopholes in 26 seconds, the lawyers took an average of 92 minutes to find 85%. The law profession may be among the first to see widespread adoption of AI[40].
- In 2017, iFlytek and Tsinghua University successfully created an AI system that scored better than over 96% of humans taking the Chinese medical licensing exam. The exam tested breadth of knowledge and the ability to understand connections between facts and use them to make decisions[41].
- AI, drones, and CCTV have been used at the Magh Mela[42], a Hindu festival attended by millions of people. CCTV counts the number of people per square metre – more than three in any one location leads to police intervention. To keep the site clean, AI-enabled cameras send a signal to a nearby lorry when a rubbish bin is full.
- AI robots are being used in Japan to replace assistant language teachers for talking to young schoolchildren in English[43]. The first commercial robot to walk on its own and climb steps is Honda's ASIMO, developed to help the elderly and disabled and used for combating fires, disarming bombs, and traversing dangerous areas[44]. The Weird Hotel in Japan is staffed by robots. Hideo Sawada, who runs the hotel, insists that using robots is a serious effort to use technology and achieve efficiency[45].

---

[1] theguardian.com – tinyurl.com/choices168
[2] "AI 'productivity revolution' will take a decade or more, say experts", *Financial Times*. June 6th, 2023
[3] Tegmark, M. *Life 3.0, Being Human in the Age of Artificial Intelligence*, Penguin. 2018
[4] Brockman, J. *Possible Minds, 25 ways of looking at AI*. Penguin Press. 2019
[5] researchgate.net – tinyurl.com/choices169
[6] sciencedirect.com – tinyurl.com/choices327

[7] "How AI can revolutionise science", *The Economist*, 16 September 2023
[8] nature.com – tinyurl.com/choices482
[9] nature.com – tinyurl.com/choices366
[10] alphafold.ebi.ac.uk – tinyurl.com/choices519
[11] nature.com – tinyurl.com/choices485
[12] bmcmededuc.biomedcentral.com – tinyurl.com/choices328
[13] bbc.co.uk – tinyurl.com/choices487
[14] Lee, K. *AI Superpowers, China, Silicon Valley and the new world order.* Houghton Mifflin Harcourt. 2019
[15] statista.com – tinyurl.com/choices215
[16] cbsnews.com – tinyurl.com/choices170
[17] wileyindustrynews.com – tinyurl.com/choices259
[18] nesta.org.uk – tinyurl.com/choices481
[19] payscale.com – tinyurl.com/choices216
[20] phys.org – tinyurl.com/choices171
[21] gov.uk – tinyurl.com/choices508
[22] justtwothings.substack.com – tinyurl.com/choices483
[23] Kahneman, D., Sibony, O., Sunstein, C.R. *Noise: A Flaw in Human Judgement.* William Collins. 2021
[24] forbes.com – tinyurl.com/choices209
[25] Private communication
[26] "AI tackling disinformation", *New Scientist*, 16 September 2023.
[27] weforum.org – tinyurl.com/choices172
[28] sites.duke.edu – tinyurl.com/choices173
[29] This experiment was in 2023: this fault may have been fixed but we hear from friends in academia that the syndrome is endemic in academic publications.
[30] Personal communication to author
[31] Webb, A. *The Big Nine: How the Tech Titans and Their Thinking Machines Could Warp Humanity.* Public Affairs. 2019
[32] news.mit.edu – tinyurl.com/choices486
[33] euronews.com – tinyurl.com/choices210
[34] "Big data may make AI more racist", *New Scientist*, 22 July 2023
[35] washingtonpost.com – tinyurl.com/choices211
[36] lordslibrary.parliament.uk – tinyurl.com/choices326
[37] weforum.org – tinyurl.com/choices212
[38] europarl.europa.eu – tinyurl.com/choices213
[39] lawsociety.ie – tinyurl.com/choices214
[40] bloomberg.com – tinyurl.com/choices322
[41] irishnews.com – tinyurl.com/choices323
[42] theweek.com – tinyurl.com/choices324
[43] japan-forward.com – tinyurl.com/choices484
[44] global.honda – tinyurl.com/choices509
[45] nypost.com – tinyurl.com/choices325

Chapter 14 – Biology

- Biology will change our lives more in the next 50 years, through gene editing, than physics has in the last 50.
- Regulation of gene editing lags behind adoption.
- In the same way that the green revolution enabled the world to feed itself, the pandemic has revolutionised the production of vaccines.

The story so far

Biology has always been a crucial part of our existence – we have been dependent on other biological species since the beginning of time.

Humans have intervened in biological processes to improve their foods and animal feeds, to tackle illness and to provide sources of energy. Humans have used animals to travel distances at speed and for lifting weights. Plants, animals and their byproducts have historically been the main source of medicines for humans. For instance, vaccines were based on living organisms: in 1796, Edward Jenner used the cowpox virus (vaccinia) to confer protection against smallpox, a related virus in humans[1].

In the last century, the use of Genetic Modification (GM) in agriculture and forestry hit the headlines. GM adds a new gene or genes to the genome of a crop plant or animal (or removes one), while traditional breeding works by crossing together species and selecting the offspring with the desired combination of characteristics[2]. Both methods are in use to improve crop yield, salt- or drought-tolerance and to provide lean meat, and to create variants of plants and animals for new places and tastes.

Thus, our dependence on biology is not new: so why did Bill Clinton say "In science, if the last 50 years were the age of physics, the next 50 years will be the age of biology"?[3]

What has happened is that a wave of innovation has revolutionised our ability to modify biological systems. The new capability to edit genes has been powered by a convergence of breakthroughs in biology, computing, data analytics, machine learning, artificial intelligence and biological engineering[4].

This chapter is mostly about understanding some of the applications of, and ethical questions raised by, gene editing.

Gene editing

The mapping of the human genome into its constituent DNA began in 1990 and was the foundation of breakthroughs in our understanding of biological structures at a cell level.

The CRISPR method for editing DNA built on this knowledge – it was unveiled in 2012; the technology was immediate and accessible. The effort needed to edit DNA decreased from 13 years and billions of dollars in 2003 to 1 day and less than $1,000 now.

Clustered Regularly Interspaced Short Palindromic Repeats (CRISPRs) occur naturally as pieces of RNA[5] copied from viruses that infect bacteria. When the CRISPR Cas9 enzyme is added to a cell with a piece of guide RNA, it hooks up with the RNA and then moves along the strands of DNA until it finds and binds to a 20-DNA-letter long sequence that matches part of the RNA sequence. The RNA then guides Cas9 to cut up the virus and usually this disables the gene[6].

CRISPR is the main tool currently used for gene editing.

Application in agriculture

Some of the many applications of gene editing include destroying a virus that lurks inside many of the bananas grown in Africa[7], improving the fat content of soya beans[8] and increasing seed size in wheat along with the production of transgene-free low-gluten wheat[9].

Other applications in view are biologically neutral cement that does not harm the environment[10], microbes designed to reduce fertiliser use[11], and a soy-based roof coating to reduce urban heat[12].

Biotech approaches to mitigating the effects of global heating include modifying the roots of cereal crops to fix nitrogen more efficiently and reduce use of inorganic fertilisers; and improving the capability of rice crops to absorb excess CO_2 in the air[13].

Applications to human health

Developments in human medicine are taking longer[14]. The recent International Summit on Human Genome Editing summarised the situation:

"Remarkable progress has been made in somatic human genome editing, demonstrating it can cure once incurable diseases. To realise its full therapeutic potential, research is needed to expand the range of diseases it can treat, and to better understand the risks and unintended effects. The extremely high costs of current somatic gene therapies are unsustainable. A global commitment to affordable, equitable access to these treatments is urgently needed.

Heritable human genome editing remains unacceptable at this time. Public discussions and policy debates continue and are important for resolving whether this technology should be used. Governance frameworks and ethical principles for the responsible use of heritable human genome editing are not in place. Necessary safety and efficacy standards have not been met."

The first gene-editing CRISPR treatment for humans, for sickle cell anaemia, was approved by the US FDA in December 2023[15, 16].

As highlighted above, the major ethical concern is about genetic editing of the germline – eggs or sperm. Changes made here will persist over generations, and the phrase 'designer baby' is used to encapsulate the concept.

During the Covid-19 pandemic, the term mRNA was increasingly heard[17], describing a new class of vaccine[18]. Covid-19 mRNA vaccines give instructions for the body's cells to make a piece of harmless 'spike protein' as found on the surface of the Covid-19 virus. The body's immune system recognises that the spike protein is foreign and begins building an immune response and making antibodies, as it would if it had actually been infected with Covid-19.

After success in delivering a Covid-19 vaccine, vaccines using mRNA delivery are being targeted at treating cancer[19]. Other new possibilities being investigated include vaccines for other infectious diseases, enzyme replacement therapy for rare diseases[20] and regenerative medicine[21]. A new technology – self activating RNA (saRNA)[22] – allows for lower doses which could help supply more vaccines quickly in a pandemic, and it is also being trialled for shingles, flu immunisation and cancer treatment.

The need for new vaccines is highlighted by CEPI[23] (Coalition for Epidemic Preparedness Innovation) which has listed sixteen bacteria and viruses that could hit the planet even harder than the Covid-19 pandemic.

Waste management and water

Biological approaches other than gene editing are being used to tackle some of the world's environmental problems.

In *Planetary Limits* we describe pollution, a worldwide problem. Plastics are a major contributor. Over the past few years, the finding of a bacterium that eats plastics[24] has led to interest in industrialising the processes to scale up its use and to develop it to work at lower temperatures. Other species which can contribute are earthworms, land-based and aquatic plants, blue-green algae, micro-organisms and fungi[25].

And while the complete desalination of water remains expensive, treating and re-using water is much more economically viable. One method for this uses a biological electrochemical system in which electro-active bacteria power the desalination of water in situ[26].

Bioengineering and biocomputing

Cyborgs[27] are often the first image that comes to mind when biotechnology is mentioned, through science fiction and increasingly in real life. Direct neural interfaces to the brain may have started with military applications but are quickly moving into wider use to tackle ageing and disability. The most famous cyborgs walking around today include people with artificial colour sensing[28], cochlear implants, prosthetic arms and bionic legs[29], artificial vision and exo-skeletons to enhance lifting[30].

And finally, for visionaries, biocomputing – the use of cells or molecules such as DNA for computation – is the subject of speculation. Calculations suggest that one kilogram of raw DNA could store all the world's data[31].

The Force for Change of *Biology* is about the development, increased application, and acceptance of gene editing. While all four Threats could disrupt this trend, the *Collapse of Global Health* is thought to have the most impact on the use of gene editing for humans.

Glimpses of change

Agriculture and food

- Researchers at Scotland's Roslin Institute have genetically modified chickens to produce proteins in egg whites for use in human medicines. Production from chickens can cost anywhere from 10 to 100 times less than in factories, and the proteins can be recovered using a simple purification system. There are no adverse effects on the chickens themselves, which lay eggs as usual[32].

Waste management

- The mystery of where plastic goes after it is dumped in the ocean has long puzzled scientists. At least fourteen million tons finds its way into marine environments each year. Now scientists believe they have solved at least part of the riddle. Bacteria are eating it. A new study by the Royal Netherlands Institute for Sea Research (NIOZ) has proven that the widespread bacterium *Rhodococcus ruber* digests plastic, turning it into carbon dioxide and other harmless substances[33].

Water

- In the Netherlands, a company has developed a biological treatment system for water in its vegetable oil processing facility, which has reduced its water use by half[34]. In Germany, the company Cereol has implemented an enzyme-based system for the degumming of vegetable oil during purification after extraction. The enzyme system has eliminated treatment with strong acid and reduced water use and waste sludge to one tenth.

Human health care

- Duchenne muscular dystrophy (DMD) is a devastating muscular disease, which greatly reduces patients' quality of life and life expectancy. Researchers in Germany have used the CRISPR gene-editing tool to correct the condition in pigs[35]. The treatment avoids one of the main issues with CRISPR gene-editing – transience: most cells in the body will die off at some point and the edited cells will eventually be replaced by cells like the original faulty ones. But heart and muscle cells are long-lived, so edits to these will have a longer effect on DMD.

---

[1] ncbi.nlm.nih.gov – tinyurl.com/choices495
[2] Chrispeels, M. J., and Gepts, P. (ed.). (2017). *Plants, Genes, and Agriculture: Sustainability through Biotechnology.* OUP USA.

[3] libquotes.com – tinyurl.com/choices510
[4] "Why the post Internet revolution is still bioscience", *Financial Times Weekend Magazine*, 9 July 2022.
[5] Ribonucleic acid, or RNA, plays a key role in turning the instructions held in DNA into functional proteins in cells. RNA is closely related to DNA.
[6] abc.net.au – tinyurl.com/choices217
[7] newscientist.com – tinyurl.com/choices174
[8] eurekalert.org – tinyurl.com/choices496
[9] ncbi.nlm.nih.gov – tinyurl.com/choices368
[10] nature.com – tinyurl.com/choices491
[11] news.mit.edu – tinyurl.com/choices218
[12] soynewuses.org – tinyurl.com/choices520
[13] isaaa.org – tinyurl.com/choices490
[14] royalsociety.org – tinyurl.com/choices219
[15] "Cut, Paste, Cure", *New Scientist*, 8 July 2023
[16] washingtonpost.com – tinyurl.com/choices175
[17] Lustig, P. and Ringland, G. *New Shoots* KDP 2021 (Out of print)
[18] genome.gov – tinyurl.com/choices497
[19] cancer.gov – tinyurl.com/choices220
[20] "Trial shows how mRNA therapies could revolutionise medicine", *New Scientist*, 3 June 2023.
[21] pubmed.ncbi.nlm.nih.gov – tinyurl.com/choices494
[22] doi.org – tinyurl.com/choices369
[23] weforum.org – tinyurl.com/choices221
[24] livescience.com – tinyurl.com/choices511
[25] Dickson, K. *Environmental Biotechnology: Easy course for understanding waste management, environmental pollution and its effects.* KDP (2017).
[26] wikiwand.com – tinyurl.com/choices493
[27] Defined as a being with both organic and biomechatronic body parts.
[28] nationalgeographic.com – tinyurl.com/choices225
[29] nbcnews.com – tinyurl.com/choices226
[30] www3.nhk.or.jp – tinyurl.com/choices176
[31] bbc.com – tinyurl.com/choices489
[32] phys.org – tinyurl.com/choices492
[33] telegraph.co.uk – tinyurl.com/choices227
[34] greentumble.com – tinyurl.com/choices488
[35] sciencedaily.com – tinyurl.com/choices367

Chapter 15 – Planetary Limits

- Water is the crucial limitation.
- Pollution, pollution, pollution is a threat to human life as well as many other species.
- Biodiversity is under threat – the next great extinction event may be looming.

The story so far

As humanity comes up against planetary limits, people are beginning to learn which limits they can do something about and which they can't. This is framed by a growing consensus that we have entered the Anthropocene[1]: an era in which human beings are the driving force behind changes to our planet.

Many assumptions about planetary limits are derived from the seminal models in *Limits to Growth,* compiled by Donella Meadows and others. This was written in 1972 and subsequently updated, most recently in 2004[2]. The report published the results of several computer models representing the world economy and society. The model's 'Business-as-Usual' Scenario projections were remarkably close to reality up to about 2015. While potential food shortages were averted through scientific advances, water and biodiversity are the resources which are hitting constraints.

Pollution is, as predicted, a major concern – see *Urban Pull*. The cities and industrial areas of Asia have dangerous levels of air, water and land pollution. Pollution was estimated in 2015 to have killed more people than the worldwide deaths recorded from the Covid-19 pandemic as we write[3]. In *Connected World* we discussed the use of Smart City technology to tackle air quality in cities.

Ocean pollution can be seen in the summer dead zone in the Gulf of Mexico. This is caused mostly by fertiliser and animal waste run-off[4]. Another famous example is in the Pacific Ocean, northeast of Hawaii, where a giant whirlpool of plastic debris has been accumulated by the ocean currents. It's referred to as the North Pacific Gyre[5] but is also commonly called 'The Great Pacific Garbage Patch'. It is approximately the size of Queensland, Australia.

Plastics are used for clothing, packaging, tools and utensils[6] and are a major source of pollution, including microparticles in the air, soil and water supply. Many of the constituent chemicals degrade with heating and can only be reused a few times[7]. So in *Biology* it will be no surprise that we included innovative ways to eat or otherwise dispose of plastics: with biological systems, for instance bacteria, tackling plastics that are polluting land and water.

Elizabeth Kolbert in *Under a White Sky*[8] takes a look at the scope of technology to save the planet. She meets biologists who are trying to preserve the world's rarest fish, which lives in a single tiny pool in the middle of the Mojave; engineers who are turning carbon emissions to stone in Iceland; Australian researchers who are trying to develop a "super coral" that can survive in hotter seas; and physicists who are contemplating shooting tiny diamonds into the stratosphere to cool the earth.

Two natural resources – biodiversity and water - are under threat as foretold in *Limits to Growth*. They are the main topic of this chapter.

Biodiversity is the existence of a wide range of species across the planet, and loss of biodiversity has unpredictable consequences. Johan Rockstrom, in *Big World, Small Planet*[9], suggests that the Earth has gone beyond restorable levels of biodiversity.

Biodiversity in Africa is declining rapidly[10]. But everywhere in the world species are diminishing. Many computer models explore examples of ecosystem collapse[11].

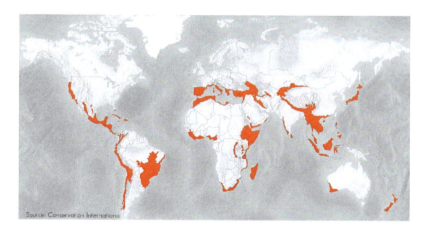

Figure 10: Biodiversity risk hotspots

Chapter 15 – Planetary Limits | 101

In *The Sixth Mass Extinction*[12], Elizabeth Kolbert argues that species loss is currently running at such a high rate that many ecosystems are threatened with collapse. The Californian bee population is suffering Colony Collapse Disease, for instance, cutting the size of crops such as almonds. We speculate that shortages of almonds, coffee or chocolate could change public attitudes to ecosystem loss. Many decision makers eat these luxury foods! Figure 10 highlights areas where biodiversity is decreasing fastest.

One of the most important ecosystems is forests. About one third of the Earth's land surface is covered by forests. The World Wide Fund for Nature (WWF) reports that half of the trees illegally removed from forests are used as fuel. Some other common reasons for cutting down forests are to make more land available for agriculture; for housing and urbanisation; and for a range of domestic and industrial uses. Most deforestation occurs in tropical rainforests. The Amazon is the biggest single forest and has lost nearly a fifth of its area in the past five decades[13]. Also by 2012, Indonesia had become the nation that cleared the most forest in the world each year[14]. It has since decreased its rate of deforestation, with a reduction of 75% by 2019[15].

Biodiversity is reduced as land is cleared for food crops. The pressure to clear land to grow food can be amplified by Global Heating. One forecast suggests that agricultural productivity will be reduced by up to a third across large parts of Africa over the next 60 years[16]. China and Saudi Arabia are leading the way in actively planning to ensure the availability of a varied range of foods for their people. This involves developing crops which can grow on land previously thought to be inhospitable and also by buying agricultural land in other countries[17].

The global trend towards meat eating as people's incomes increase is a source of pressure on wild habitats, especially in Africa and Asia. Research[18] carried out at the University of Oxford suggests that producing cultured beef in a laboratory could require as little as 1% of the space required by current livestock farming methods. Of course, laboratory beef also requires energy and water; it produces a different mix of Greenhouse Gases and may turn out to have unhealthy characteristics. So, as with other choices, there are trade-offs to be considered.

And what about water?

The types of food increasingly demanded as people's incomes rise – dairy, meat and fish – require large amounts of clean water. Water is a resource that has traditionally been taken for granted. Although many rivers in Europe have become cleaner and been restocked with wildlife[19], farming continues to pollute many[20]. Meanwhile, many rivers elsewhere are undergoing the same degradation that rivers in the global north did during the 19th-century industrial revolution[21]. And shortage of drinking water is already here, as demonstrated in Cape Town in 2017/18[22] and by the stresses in the western USA[23] in more recent years. Safe drinking water remains out of reach for billions[24].

In *The Atlas of Water*[25], Maggie Black identifies areas of water shortage, as shown in Figure 11. In the Figure, physical water scarcity means that there is physically not enough water for the population. Economic water scarcity is different because while there may be enough water physically present, it is either too expensive to buy or clean resulting in water insecurity.

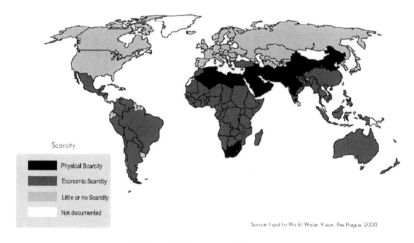

Figure 11: Water shortage 2025[26]

Water Shortage 2025

Based on current trends, by 2030, worldwide freshwater withdrawals are expected to exceed reliable supplies by nearly half. Maggie Black highlights North Africa and the Middle East, China, India and Pakistan as being particularly under pressure. This is due to increasing populations, rising living standards and the falling water levels of their rivers and water tables. Erratic weather patterns due to global warming are also increasing the probability of water shortages in vulnerable areas, as we discussed in *Global Heating*.

Technology is being used to address the worldwide shortage of drinkable water and also to tackle local shortages with methods such as waterless soap and washing machines and toilets that use little or no water. Desalination is expensive and energy intensive and is currently a last option[27]. Crops that grow in saline water are increasingly part of the economy in dry areas: the government of the Netherlands reports a breakthrough in food security as some varieties of potatoes, carrots, red onions, white cabbage and broccoli appear to thrive if they are irrigated with salt water[28]. In *Biology* we include some examples of the role of genetic engineering in providing new sources of food.

Currently, half of the world's population endures extremely high water stress at least one month of the year – a number the Water Resource Institute predicts will rise to 60% by 2050[29]. Water is probably the most crucial natural resource and there is no apparent plan B. The year 2023 marked the first major conference of the United Nations dedicated to water since 1977. Sustainable Development Goal 6 (SDG 6) is to ensure availability and sustainable management of water and sanitation for all by 2030. At current rates, progress towards all the targets of SDG 6 is off-track and in some areas the rate of implementation needs to quadruple, or more[30].

Planetary Limits is about further loss of biodiversity and increasing water shortages. We suggest that *Breakdown of International Relations* due to the damage to the environment caused by conflict and war, and *Collapse of Global Health* due to AMR's effects on humans, animals, the environment and the food chain, are the Threats likely to have the most (negative) impact on these trends.

What can be learnt from the Green Revolution? This has allowed the world to feed itself, through a combination of public awareness, globally based scientific advances[31] and support from governments. Are there signs of public awareness, global scientific co-operation or support from governments to tackle biodiversity loss?

Glimpses of change

Adapting to water shortages

- Waterless Limited[32] makes a specially formulated range of 'Towel Off' shampoos and soaps, Nilaqua, that allow you to wash effectively without water or rinsing. The concept was originally developed to enable astronauts to wash in space. Nilaqua is now used for people who are disabled, or bed bound, who cannot wash traditionally. It is also used after natural disasters such as the earthquakes in 2011 in

Japan, where running water was not available, and for personal hygiene in the South African water crisis. Using Nilaqua allowed people to have more of their ration available for drinking and cooking. Finally, it also reduces waste such as baby wipes and shampoo caps, as it provides multiple washes per bottle and the bottles are recyclable.

Pollution

- Japanese scientists have demonstrated the use of bacteria to 'eat' previously non-biodegradable plastic bags and bottles. This approach could be a major contribution to cleaning up the oceans[33].

Biodiversity

- Vertical ocean farming allows coastal areas to recover. One scheme, by GreenWave, is for seaweed, scallops and mussels to grow on floating ropes that are stacked above oyster and clam cages below. An acre can grow 10-30 tons of sea vegetables and 250,000 shellfish each year. Their training site for potential developers is at Thimble Island, Connecticut[34].
- The rare large blue butterfly is now flying in the UK on a Cotswold hillside after 150 years' absence. About 750 butterflies emerged on Rodborough Common in 2020 after 1,100 larvae were released. This followed five years of innovative grassland management to create the optimum habitat. Its return to Britain is a successful insect reintroduction project, after caterpillars were initially brought from Sweden in an ecologist's camper van[35]. China has doubled the number of wild animals protected under its conservation rules. The government has imposed hefty fines on the trading and consumption of 500 species, including many birds and wolves. It comes after 30 years of Chinese environmental groups fighting for animals to be added to the protected list. The groups hope that the ban will also help to combat international trafficking of wild animals[36].

---

[1] "The Anthropocene Era", *The Week*, 9 September 2023
[2] clubofrome.org – tinyurl.com/choices521

[3] Pollution linked to 9 million deaths worldwide in 2015, study says | CNN – tinyurl.com/choices459

[4] oceantoday.noaa.gov – tinyurl.com/choices463

[5] education.nationalgeographic.org – tinyurl.com/choices458

[6] "How plastics took over the modern world", *The Week*, 26 August 2023

[7] "The Long Road", *The Week*, 26 August 2023

[8] Kolbert, E. *Under a White Sky.* Vintage, 2022

[9] stockholmresilience.org – tinyurl.com/choices177

[10] controlrisks.com – tinyurl.com/choices178

[11] nature.com – tinyurl.com/choices498

[12] Kolbert, E. *The Sixth Extinction: An Unnatural History,* Bloomsbury, 2014

[13] worldwildlife.org – tinyurl.com/choices455

[14] pbs.org – tinyurl.com/choices321

[15] earth.org – tinyurl.com/choices456

[16] phys.org – tinyurl.com/choices391

[17] middleeasteye.net – tinyurl.com/choices320

[18] ox.ac.uk – tinyurl.com/choices319

[19] eea.europa.eu – inyurl.com/choices392

[20] "A very mucky problem", *New Scientist,* 24 June 2023

[21] theguardian.com – tinyurl.com/choices180

[22] weforum.org – tinyurl.com/choices318

[23] "Learning from the Dust Bowl", *Scientific American,* July 2021

[24] "Safe drinking water remains out of reach for billions", *New Scientist,* 1 April 2023

[25] Black, M. *The Atlas of Water,* Routledge, 2009

[26] reddit.com – tinyurl.com/choices179

[27] sciencedirect.com – tinyurl.com/choices370

[28] government.nl – tinyurl.com/choices181

[29] wri.org – tinyurl.com/choices182

[30] unwater.org – tinyurl.com/choices457

[31] pnas.org – tinyurl.com/choices460

[32] https://waterlessltd.co.uk/

[33] theguardian.com – tinyurl.com/choices317

[34] https://www.greenwave.org/our-model

[35] bbc.com – tinyurl.com/choices461

[36] nature.com – tinyurl.com/choices462

Chapter 16 – Economic Activity

- Poverty has decreased globally and the centre of economic activity has moved to Asia[1].
- People are starting to think that just GDP growth is not enough.
- Technology has disrupted economic models and the ability of governments to control their own economy.

The story so far

Over recent decades, many people have moved out of poverty. Figure 12 shows that in 1800, most people were poor, living below the poverty line. (The new international poverty line was set at $2.15 using 2017 prices by the World Bank in 2022[2]). By 1975, most people in Europe and North America were above the poverty line, but most people in Asia and Africa were still below it. By 2015, most people were above the poverty line[3].

Today, less than one billion people do not have electricity stable enough to run a refrigerator[4]. There are about a billion people at Economic Level 4 (see Appendix 2) which is likely to include most of our readers.

How has this happened?

The move to towns and cities discussed in *Urban Pull* has been one of the biggest changes. Productivity – which supports the creation of wealth – is higher in urban than rural areas[5]. Improved public health – particularly water supply and sanitation – has meant that more babies survive to adulthood, so there have been more people of working age. Meanwhile, food production has increased and supply is more stable due to the Green Revolution, as we discussed in *Planetary Limits*. Education and literacy levels have increased, so that over the 200 years since 1820, the percentage of the population that can both read and write has gone from 10% to 90%[6].

By 2040, the majority of people are expected to be at Economic Levels 3 and 4[7]. The bulk of this growth is expected to come from Asia. The world is seen as dividing into two parts: one part is mostly countries in Europe and the Americas, with slow economic growth and a shrinking workforce. The other part, mostly in Africa and Asia, has high economic growth. This is often referred to as the shift from West to East, or from the Global North to the

Majority World. Roughly one third of the world has a shrinking workforce supporting a growing number of older people[8] and China's low birthrate is quickly causing it to face a declining workforce[9] and slowing growth[10].

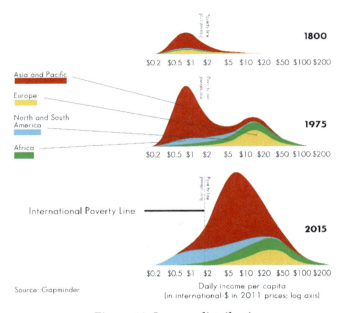

Figure 12: Income distribution

The shift will change the shape of innovation to focus on the needs and wants of the growing economies. From consumer goods to heavy machinery, the shift to the East changes not only where goods and services are developed and built, but also their standards and style[11].

This shift masks a more complex picture occurring within the labour force. Three structural forces have altered the basis of wages and the trajectory of moves out of poverty[12].

First, manual effort has been largely replaced in farming, manufacturing, transport and construction.

Second, the humans who did the work originally provided process control and the knowledge and know-how for production. Increasingly, this knowledge and know-how are embodied in the plant and equipment, which is highly specialised and also easily replicated.

Third, where raw materials are mined or grown, extraction and farming are becoming automated – and raw materials are increasingly being replaced by materials manufactured using automated processes.

Together, these change the structure of human societies, reducing the power of the labour force. The shift from the power of labour to the power of platforms means that some jobs do not add enough value to provide an adequate income to support workers, even though the price of some goods such as food and clothing is reduced from historic levels[13]. Some governments have introduced top-up payments to tackle this gap[14].

Platforms have many benefits for organisations and individuals who can take advantage of them. Many of these do not make the headlines, but for instance ICT platforms for freelancers enable remote work across continents[15], much software development is done by remote teams[16], 68% of all travel and tourism was booked online in 2022[17], and blockchain is set to reduce the paperwork of cross-border trading[18].

In the manufacturing sector much of the economic impact of 3D printing is not yet visible[19], but it is a technology to watch.

Social media platforms gained new users during the Covid-19 pandemic. This accelerated some existing employment trends, such as Working from Home and remote business meetings, supported by improving ICT networks. As a consequence, many cities are reshaping, with reduced central office space and property prices. The discussion of several types of ICT-based platforms in *Connected World* illustrated the range of applications.

Many white-collar jobs as we knew them are vanishing, as platforms and AI replace some of the functions of knowledge workers[20]. One suggestion for the future of work is that 1 billion people will be in traditional full-time paid employment out of a population of 8.5 billion[21] by 2050. Another is that by 2030, intelligent agents[22] and robots could replace 800 million jobs worldwide, mostly blue- and white-collar jobs[23]. A third estimate is that one in seven jobs (66 million) in OECD countries is "highly automatable"[24].

In richer countries many jobs and much of the economic value produced are already in the services sector. Middle income countries have over the past decades looked to follow a similar industrialisation route based on export of manufactured goods, followed by growth of services in the domestic economy. However, increased specialisation has meant that the trickle-down effect of this is reducing, and that the workforce leaving rural areas will increasingly be absorbed in lower value, small-scale services[25].

Underpinning ICT-based platforms are the relatively few big tech companies based in China and the USA. Their regulation is weak in four areas[26]: safety, privacy, competition, and honesty. It is suggested by Shoshana Zuboff and others that, "In big tech we face a totalising power that in key respects disqualifies itself from being understood as capitalism, but rather as a wholly new form of governance by the few over the many."[27]

These are some of the factors which are leading to *Social Change*.

Overall, at the same time as global average incomes converge, there is a trend towards increased inequality within a country. Inequality within countries has been correlated with societal problems leading to crises and revolution[28]. Figure 13 shows how global inequality affects people's living conditions. Countries with high income inequality have a high index of health and social problems. At the other extreme, low income inequality and low rates of health and social problems are correlated[29].

Figure 13: Living conditions and inequality[30]

Many economists believe that the divisions between rich and poor individuals – and nations – are unsustainable. A Universal Basic Income is proposed by, among others, the World Economic Forum[31] to reduce the effect of poverty on health and education. Oliver Bullough's *Moneyland* argues that the increased mobility of money and the large percentage of wealth in private (rather than government) hands, means that the international financial system is unlikely to survive in its current form[32].

At the same time, flows of people and money across many borders are easy, are increasing and are difficult for nation states to control. The flows are large: for instance, cross-border remittances from one currency to another are now as important as foreign direct investment to many lower and middle income countries[33]. Supply chains extending over many firms and countries mean that organisations can choose to recognise revenue in low tax locations.

Capitalism has been a factor in the movement of large numbers of people out of poverty: so why is it thought to be in trouble? The symptoms are often cited as: societies with high inequality and degraded democracy; firms with feeble productivity; weak competition; headlines on fraud and tax evasion; and an imbalance between the powers of investors and consumers[34]. The book *Silent Coup* provides a number of examples of the distorting effect of large corporates on local and national economies – with a diminution of the capability of government. The US trials of big tech company Google accuse it of abusing its online search monopoly to extract bigger profits, snuff out competition and slow innovation: most countries are not of a size or economic power to challenge such a large and profitable organisation[35].

As Churchill famously said, "Democracy is the worst form of government, except for all the others." Might capitalism be in a similar condition? That is, the worst form of economic management, except for all the others? We will pick this up in the next chapter, *Social Change*. And in *Fractured Backbones* we cited the recognition by the World Bank of the need to alleviate poverty on a liveable planet, by tackling climate change, food insecurity and pandemics[36].

One of the ideas which has contributed to public awareness of resource limitations is the circular economy: a model based on the circular economy and planetary limits is Doughnut Economics[37].

The model embeds the economy in the Earth's systems and in society, including the flow of materials and energy. It includes people as more than just workers, consumers and owners of capital. The inner ring of the doughnut represents a sufficiency of the resources for a decent life: sufficient food, clean water, housing, sanitation, energy, education, healthcare and good government. Meanwhile the billion people in the hole in the middle of the doughnut do not have the basics, have limited choices and their lives are precarious. The outer boundary is more fluid. Humans have breached it in several places by using up or degrading resources faster than they can be replenished by planetary environmental ecosystems – we discussed biodiversity in *Planetary Limits*.

Recycling and resources usage is becoming of interest – not least because of concern over the stability of supply chains. Thinking has moved on from sending waste for recycling to Asia[38], to new wealth creation businesses which – for example – "de-produce" cars rather than scrapping them[39].

By DoughnutEconomics - Own work, CC BY-SA 4.0,
https://commons.wikimedia.org/w/index.php?curid=75695171

Figure 14: The Doughnut of social and planetary boundaries [40]

The trend towards fewer people living in poverty may be harder to maintain at the same speed over the next decades, as a decreasing fraction of the world is living in poverty. The Threats to the continuation of the trend of decreasing numbers of people in poverty are *Fractured Backbones* and *Breakdown of International Relations*.

Glimpses of change

Reduction in poverty

- Bangladesh is home to 160 million people. Since 1991, GDP per capita has increased seven-fold – at its current growth rate, Bangladesh is on track to become an upper-middle-income country with at least $4,000 GDP per capita by 2031[41]. 24 million people have been lifted out of poverty, life expectancy has risen to 72 years[42], infant and maternal mortality rates have fallen by a factor of five and the literacy rate has increased from one third to three quarters[43]. This has happened due to the rise of a middle class, technological advancement and financial inclusion, infrastructure, exports, and the important role of remittances into the rural areas[44].

Resource use

- In downtown Bordeaux, Mireille Paumier repairs many things. She replaces buttons and jacket linings, renews broken seams, changes waistbands and skirt waists, plugs holes or patches them with a piece of fabric. Now, Ms. Paumier's work will be supported by the French government, which has set up a fund for clothing repairs, paid financed by France's fashion industry. Since 2023, anyone in France who has shoes resoled or clothing repaired receives a repair bonus of between €6 and €25, to encourage consumers to visit cobblers and tailors instead of throwing away old shoes and clothes. Some €154 million is available for the programme until 2028[45].

Reducing inequality

- The Covid-19 outbreak is a good example to explore the impact of less inequality[46]. In some countries, such as South Korea and New Zealand, inequality and the other pressures had been kept largely at bay. Trust in government and social cohesion was also generally higher. When the disease appeared, people in these countries were able to pull together and respond more effectively than elsewhere. They quickly managed to implement an array of strategies to fight the disease, like masking and physical distancing guidelines, that were supported and followed by large numbers of people. And generally, there was a fairly swift response from leaders in these countries with the state providing financial support for missed work, organising food drives and setting up other crucial programmes to help people manage with all of the disruptions Covid brought[47].
- The M-Pesa example in *Connected World* is a good precedent[48].

New sources of income

- Every year, millions of tonnes of electronic waste including old laptops, mobile phones and televisions are thrown away. However, The Royal Mint – whose job it is to make coins for the UK – has come up with a unique way to turn these items, which are collectively known as e-waste, into something valuable. It has started using new technology to recover gold from recycled electronic products: taking the circuit boards from old mobiles and computers and extracting the precious metal by putting the boards through high temperature chemical processes. At the moment, the Royal Mint is focusing on extracting gold from e-waste, but it hopes to recover a number of other metals including copper, silver, tin and nickel.[49]

Regulating big tech

- In 2024, the US Department of Justice, and the Biden White House in general, was working hard to understand how to be effective. The New Brandeis school of legal theory – of which the DoJ's current antitrust division head, Jonathan Kanter, Federal Trade Commission chair Lina Khan and former White House antitrust adviser Tim Wu are part — is built on the idea that power exists in the political economy and it can't be modelled algorithmically. To them, "antitrust law is something that belongs to the public, not judges or an elite legal fraternity", says Matt Stoller, the director of research at the American Economic Liberties Project. That's why it's so important that in its second major antitrust case filed against Google, the US Department of Justice asked not only that the company break up its advertising business, but that a jury of the people decide whether it must do so. This is extremely unusual for antitrust cases, which are usually decided by a judge[50].

---

[1] gapminder.org – tinyurl.com/choices512
[2] worldbank.org – tinyurl.com/choices301
[3] gapminder.org – tinyurl.com/choices302
[4] ourworldindata.org – tinyurl.com/choices499
[5] sciencedirect.com – tinyurl.com/choices316
[6] Source: Our World in Data based on Zanden, J. et al. (2014) via OECD and UNESCO via World Bank OurWorldInData.org/literacy • CC BY
[7] gapminder.org – tinyurl.com/choices522
[8] See *Population*
[9] "A crisis of confidence", *The Economist*, 19 August 2023
[10] reuters.com – tinyurl.com/choices303

[11] Prahalad, C. K. *The Fortune at the Bottom of the Pyramid; Eradicating Poverty Through Profits.* Financial Times/ Prentice Hall (2004).

[12] Boulding, K. E. "The Economics of Knowledge and the Knowledge of Economics." *The American Economic Review*, vol. 56, no. 1/2, 1966, pp. 1–13. JSTOR

[13] onlinelibrary.wiley.com – tinyurl.com/choices371

[14] bbc.co.uk – tinyurl.com/choices500

[15] independant.io – tinyurl.com/choices513

[16] gartner.com – tinyurl.com/choices311

[17] dreambigtravelfarblog.com – tinyurl.com/choices382

[18] juniperresearch.com – tinyurl.com/choices386

[19] zdnet.com – tinyurl.com/choices312

[20] theguardian.com – tinyurl.com/choices313

[21] millennium-project.org – tinyurl.com/choices299

[22] Entities that use sensors to perceive the environment, make a decision, and act upon that information using actuators, study.com – tinyurl.com/choices310

[23] cnbc.com – tinyurl.com/choices298

[24] oecd.org – tinyurl.com/choices300

[25] project-syndicate.org – tinyurl.com/choices314

[26] time.com – tinyurl.com/choices385

[27] theguardian.com – tinyurl.com/choices315

[28] theconversation.com – tinyurl.com/choices231

[29] Pickett, K. and Wilkinson, J. *The Spirit Level: Why equality is better for everyone,* Penguin. 2010

[30] Max Roser (2019) "Global Inequality of Opportunity", OurWorldInData.org – tinyurl.com/choices228

[31] weforum.org – tinyurl.com/choices309

[32] Bullough, O. *Moneyland: Why Thieves And Crooks Now Rule The World And How To Take It Back* Profile books, 2018

[33] weforum.org – tinyurl.com/choices384

[34] Provost, C. and Kennard, M. *Silent Coup: How corporations overthrew democracy,* Bloomsbury, 2023

[35] "The DoJ's search showdown", *The Economist*, 16 September 2023.

[36] "Stretching the World Bank's balance sheet", Gillian Tett, *Financial Times* 29 September 2023

[37] Raworth, K. *Doughnut Economics: A model for organising economic activity so that people thrive,* Random House Business 2018. Also tinyurl.com/choices389

[38] standard.co.uk – tinyurl.com/choices308

[39] "Can we create a circular motor industry?", *New Scientist,* 20 May 2023

[40] Anne E Urai, Clare Kelly (2023) Point of View: Rethinking academia in a time of climate crisis. elifesciences.org – tinyurl.com/choices230
[41] bcg.com – tinyurl.com/choices307
[42] knoema.com – tinyurl.com/choices387
[43] macrotrends.net – tinyurl.com/choices229
[44] businessinspection.com – tinyurl.com/choices383
[45] reasonstobecheerful.world – tinyurl.com/choices306
[46] coronavirus.jhu.edu – tinyurl.com/choices514
[47] theconversation.com – tinyurl.com/choices305
[48] mckinsey.com – tinyurl.com/choices304
[49] bbc.co.uk – tinyurl.com/choices388
[50] ft.com – tinyurl.com/choices372

Chapter 17 – Social Change

- Over the past decades, the pace and extent of social and economic change has made many people feel uncertain.
- ICT and social media platforms are changing people's assumptions about everything – including the nature of governance and the balance of power between countries, businesses and people.
- Democracy is being challenged by authoritarianism.

The story so far

The forces for change described so far have already caused massive social change, with big shifts in the economy and society. It has become clear that many shared assumptions are no longer valid.

Within the next 20 years, the next generation will face new paradigms. Where and how people work is changing; the number of children women have is decreasing; populations are ageing; and a growing percentage of the global population can exercise the power of choice. The next wave of crisis in *Global Heating* is approaching fast, and any of the four Threats identified in Part One can disrupt things at any time. The impact of technology – ICT and Biology - is set to increase over the next decades. Migration is becoming a major Force for Change, with large movements of people across the globe.

Here we recap on some of the forces causing social change before looking at the resulting challenges to governance; this prompts us to ask – what could new governance models look like?

Social change causes uncertainty

People who until recently had felt in control of their lives, now believe that the rules have changed. It is likely that they aren't sure what the new rules are. This is creating uncertainty, so that they are stressed and may carry suppressed anger[1].

Many things contribute to people's feelings of uncertainty. As described in *Population*, what 'family' means is being redefined, as households are increasingly made up of a single person, or even groups of unrelated people. The impact of this on society is profound – assumptions embedded in many welfare schemes are that there will be family support for children and for older or vulnerable people. These assumptions are no longer valid in many places[2].

Family connections have often been the basis of finding employment as well as underpinning many social connections. With fewer family members, people are finding that they need to depend on other types of relationships: with people living nearby, through education, shared interests, or increasingly through participation in virtual communities. As described in *Urban Pull*, one of the successes of cities is the thousands of voluntary commitments between people with no traditional family ties.

Some regions have fast-growing economies and populations, others have declining populations and low or no economic growth, as described in *Economic Activity*. In the same way that many manual jobs have disappeared, middle-class jobs are being semi- or completely automated. The headlines are about AI and jobs, but already the middle-management layers of most organisations are hollowed out. This means that Generation Z and Millennials are likely to need to develop new skills and to consider different careers[3], as described in *AI*.

Covid-19 exposed cracks in the economy and in society, accelerated some Forces for Change and disrupted others. Education of children and young people has been disrupted, putting the future of a generation at risk. Children, especially girls, may not return to school. Socialisation stopped with lockdown and when school resumed, it was not necessarily the same.

Lockdowns changed how people work and led to people taking stock. Some chose to improve their work/life balance by down-shifting and changing jobs, some chose to retire early, and others opted for working from home rather than in the office, with results described in *Economic Activity*.

As an example, Chinese people born in the 1990s and 2000s are behaving differently from their parents. China's economy is stagnating and the unemployment rate for 16-24-year-olds in cities is 21%. The mood is of *tangping* (lying flat) and *bailan* (letting it rot). A small but growing number of well-educated young Chinese seem likely to abandon their country. However most young Chinese will stay at home: the danger is that they could become infected with nihilistic nationalism[4].

Technology as a source of social change

ICT is embedded in most of our lives. It can provide benefits, as described in *Connected World*. But it can also be disenfranchising – for instance the elderly who are not IT literate are having to deal with banking that is increasingly only available online[5].

In *Economic Activity* we described some of the structural changes in the workforce due to ICT which have led to social change. AI will cause further social transformation as professions are changed through large language models (see *AI*).

Less visibly, ICT applied to Biology is likely to be a paradigm changer (see *Planetary Limits* and *Biology*). As for *AI*, attempts to regulate development in biology lag behind technological capability.

It is also useful to think about the effect of *Mobility* on social change: migration is underpinned by the ability to move yourself and your family to find a better life: so the affordability and availability of travel is enabling social change amongst large numbers of migrants heading for the USA and Europe, and within Asia.

Daniel Susskind in *Growth: A Reckoning*[6] discusses some consequences of economic growth over the past two centuries. While it has freed billions from poverty and ill health, the world now has deepening inequalities, destabilising technologies, environmental destruction and climate change. He suggests that, while there are signs that the world is hitting physical limits, innovation and technology can provide an opportunity to create a society that addresses these issues.

Challenges to governments and governance

Today's governments are largely based on place – national or local. But most people (and money) are now mobile – across national borders or from country to town. The rules of where you may vote are often disconnected from where you pay taxes on income or expenditure. The connection between paying taxes and gaining benefits is being reduced and this reduces the legitimacy of governments and their ability to support their citizens. As Oliver Bullough says "The very wealthiest people … have tunnelled into this new land that lies beneath all our nation states, where borders have vanished. They move their money … and themselves wherever they wish, picking and choosing which countries' laws they wish to live by."[7]

The myths and metaphors of the Global North have dominated for the past century. The shift in power to Asia that we described in *Economic Activity* means that different worldviews and assumptions about relationships, politics, business, and economic and social systems are informing global decisions. This has highlighted the cracks in mature societies and the stresses to democracy and capitalism.

Democratic politics is likely to change as Generation Z and Millennials start to dominate the workforce. They are more likely to vote electronically if permitted and to take advantage of citizen engagement through referenda or citizens' assemblies[8]. They are capable of organising across geographic boundaries to solve problems and capable of moving to find a culture they are comfortable with[9]. They are redefining the meaning of community, as they use social media to organise.

However, globally, democracy is in retreat[10]. The Democracy Index 2021 found that less than half the world lived in a democracy. Methods and organising principles of democracy vary. For instance participatory democracy practices (information, consultation, dialogue and partnership) have different models to organise participation; and communitarian countries like Germany, France, Japan, and Singapore emphasise the creation, maintenance, or expression of the reality of community[11]. President Barack Obama gave voice to communitarian ideas and ideals in his book *The Audacity of Hope*[12], and during the 2008 presidential election campaign he repeatedly called upon Americans to "ground our politics in the notion of a common good" for an "age of responsibility", and for foregoing identity politics in favour of community-wide unity building. Liberal democracy, a form of democracy in which the power of government is limited, and the freedom and rights of individuals are protected by constitutionally established norms and institutions, is the predominant form of democracy. It may seem messy, and add to uncertainty.

Democracies are struggling to cope[13]. Hamish McRae in *The World in 2050* says, "The legitimacy of the leadership derives from the voters. But the leaders don't do what the people want, and despise them for their primitive views.[14]" McRae goes on to note that most democracies aren't well managed, and there is a wide variance between those few countries that have the skills to formulate effective policy and implement it well, and the rest.

What else if not democracy?

The future of democracy is likely to depend on the systems adopted by Asian nations, as their political power increases in line with their increasing economic strength. There is evidence that respect for democratic ideals is declining across Asia[15]: the World Values Survey provides only partial endorsement of the idea that basic values tend to converge as people get richer[16]. On measure after measure – from thinking that children ought to be obedient, to tolerance of homosexuality, to agreeing that "when religion and science conflict, religion is always right"– Europeans and Americans have moved in the direction of greater individualism and secularism in the past 25 years. Meanwhile Orthodox, Islamic and Latin American countries have seen either smaller changes or, in some cases, movement towards more traditionalism and collectivism. That does not necessarily invalidate the idea that global values will one day converge. But it does suggest that day may be some way off.

The countries that are now emerging as powerful economies have different myths and metaphors from the Global North. The rising number of middle-class people, especially in Asia, has shown that structures other than democracy can provide improvement in people's standard of living (and allow them to become middle class). In particular, one rather different system has emerged.

The authoritarian/managerial approach is epitomised by China. China's success in achieving relatively high levels of economic development while further centralising power under authoritarian one-party rule has offered an attractive alternative to Western liberal democracy for many autocrats both inside and outside Asia[17].

In 2022, a report[18] found that half of the world's democracies were suffering worsening civil liberties and rule of law, while already authoritarian governments were becoming more oppressive.

Accepting that people may have different assumptions about the economy and society can be a challenge. However, if people are willing to talk to each other, they can find ways to work to get along and identify where they agree to disagree. Disputes can be resolved peacefully. Then they can move on to work to identify win/win opportunities, and to develop a positive vision for the future. This will create the best opportunity for finding the energy for change and thus improving everyone's lives.

Increased connectivity means that more people are encountering cultures new to them. Innovative forces are released as different worldviews and cultures intersect. This contributes to uncertainty but is also an opportunity for positive change. Multipolarity can make worldwide business harder to conduct if people struggle to understand each other's worldviews and culture. Yet the added diversity can enable increased potential for innovation, creativity and growth[19].

The undesirable characteristics of our world over the past decades have been widely commented on. Change seems possible. Now we have an opportunity to ask: what would a desirable society look like?

Models for desirable societies

A number of authors have proposed frameworks for achieving desirable future societies. Here are some examples:

Ziauddin Sardar's discussion of "Post-normal Times"[20] emphasises that, at the end of an era, "to have any notion of a viable future, we must grasp the significance of this period of transition which is characterised by three c's: complexity, chaos and contradictions. The way forward must be based on virtues of humility, modesty and accountability, the indispensable requirement of living with uncertainty, complexity and ignorance. We have to imagine ourselves into a new age of normality — with an ethical compass and a broad spectrum of imaginations from the rich diversity of human cultures".

Kate Raworth's *Doughnut Economics*[21] zeroes in on a system that meets the world's needs without exhausting the planet. She advances Seven Principles[22]:

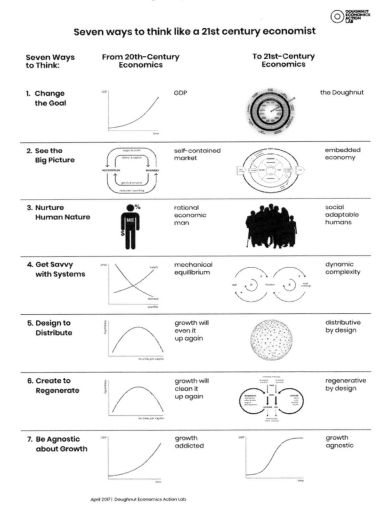

Figure 15: Seven Ways to think like a 21st-century economist

Paul Collier and John Kay's book, *Greed Is Dead: Politics After Individualism*[23], argues that community and mutuality will be the drivers of successful societies in the future – as they are already in some parts of the world. They show how politics can reverse the move to extremes of right and left of recent years, that the centre can hold and that if people think differently, the resulting common ground can benefit all.

Gillian Tett's book, *Anthro-Vision*[24], explains how a qualitative understanding of who people are and what they care about is vital to rebuilding a more equal world. She argues that to solve 21st-century problems, people must expand their fields of vision and fill in old blind spots with new empathy. By applying the techniques of anthropology that she learned as a young scholar in Cambridge and Tajikistan, she aims to understand our own familiar yet strange tribe.

We also find the African approach of Ubuntu[25] instructive. In an Ubuntu setting there is no 'private dispute' of any seriousness, since a dispute affects everyone in one way or another. As the African philosopher Mbiti says, the philosophy is based on the "I am because we are, because we are, therefore I am" principle. There is recognition of the importance of relationship and harmony in the community.

The *Social Change* Force for Change describes changing economic models, ongoing social change, and competing governance models.

The impact of *Global Heating* could be to accelerate social change as lifestyles change and people move away from areas affected by extreme weather and local climate change.

Breakdown of International Relations frequently accelerates social change which is often negative in the short term. *Collapse of Global Health* can indirectly cause surprising social change, as when virtual connections took off in organisations previously dependent on face-to-face meetings, during the Covid-19 pandemic (see *Connected World*).

Glimpses of change

Social Change - immigration

- A Glimpse of success stories of immigrants to Canada can be found in *Population*.

- Heman Bekele immigrated to America from Ethiopia as a four-year-old. Only ten years later, 3M awarded Heman the prize for America's

Top Young Scientist. Heman created a soap "with compounds that could reactivate the cells that guard human skin, enabling them to fight cancer cells."[26]

- Miguel Mbinowa Ngnobidadji emigrated from Cameroon to France and explains "My life back in Cameroon was not a great one. I grew up very poor and life in the village was hard. I couldn't afford school. If I had work, I would not have left my country. But when things are not going well and you feel stuck, you are forced to leave for better opportunities elsewhere, no matter the cost. It's not a matter of choice, it's a matter of survival. I am happy with my new life in France. I have all the things that I used to dream of: a job, a house, a car, access to public and social services — I am comfortable. I may not be at home, but I feel at home here. I spend most of my time working because for me, work is a luxury and something I take seriously"[27].

Technology

- A Glimpse reflecting the use of technology in *Social Change* was the millennials' response to the Nepal earthquake, in *Connected World*.
- Another Glimpse reflecting the contribution of technology to *Social Change* was the way that in Africa, M-Pesa has revolutionised access to finance using mobile phones, see *Connected World*.
- Another is the use of cryptocurrency in developing nations to help tackle corruption, through its transparent structure, see *Connected World*.
- A Glimpse of measures by the US Government to regulate technology companies is part of *Economic Activity*.

Governance and governments

- Ukrainians have many aspirations for their country. They look for an end to Russian intervention in Ukraine's politics and a clean government. But their fundamental demand is one that has motivated people over many decades to take a stand against corrupt, abusive and autocratic governments. They want a rules-based democracy. It is easy to understand why. Democracies are on average richer than non-democracies, are less likely to go to war and have a better record of fighting corruption. More fundamentally, democracy lets people speak their minds and shape their own and their children's futures. That so many people in so many different parts of the world are prepared to risk so much for this idea is testimony to its enduring appeal[28].

- Aruba is a small densely populated island in the Caribbean, inhabited by 100,000 Dutch citizens. From 2010 to 2012, conversations including more than half the population developed a strategic plan, *Nos Aruba 2025*. This had three positive outcomes. First were the conversations that took place across cultures and generations. Second, the plan tackled issues such as sustainability. Third, the most profound impact was a vision transformed into a manageable and feasible plan that the community pro-actively implemented. This reflected a change to an adult-adult political conversation.[29,30]

- In July 2016, the Irish Parliament approved the setting up of The Citizens' Assembly of Ireland 2016-2018. This was tasked to consider important national matters such as how best to respond to the challenges and opportunities of an aging population; how the state can make Ireland a leader in tackling climate change; and the manner in which future referenda are held[31]. The most recent Citizens' Assembly was on the loss of biodiversity.

---

[1] peopletweaker.com – tinyurl.com/choices380
[2] theguardian.com – tinyurl.com/choices295
[3] globalnews.ca – tinyurl.com/choices291 & theguardian.com – tinyurl.com/choices292
[4] scmp.com – tinyurl.com/choices294
[5] ageuk.org.uk – tinyurl.com/choices290
[6] Susskind, D., *Growth: A Reckoning*, Penguin, 2024
[7] Bullough, O., *Moneyland*, St Martins Publishing Group, 2020
[8] theconversation.com – tinyurl.com/choices293
[9] "Getting out", *The Economist*, 2 September 2023
[10] eiu.com – tinyurl.com/choices379
[11] academic.oup.com – tinyurl.com/choices287
[12] Obama, B., *The Audacity of Hope*, Canongate Books, 2007
[13] "How to make democracy faster", *Financial Times Weekend*, 1 October 2023

[14] McRae, H. *The World in 2050: How to think about the future*, Bloomsbury, 2022

[15] "Asian democracy is declining", *The Economist*. 2 September 2023

[16] "People's principles were expected to align as countries got richer. What happened?" *The Economist*, 12 August 2023

[17] birmingham.ac.uk – tinyurl.com/choices286

[18] euronews.com – tinyurl.com/choices285

[19] mckinsey.com – tinyurl.com/choices296 & scientificamerican.com – tinyurl.com/choices297

[20] ziauddinsardar.com – tinyurl.com/choices378

[21] Raworth, K. *Doughnut Economics: Seven Ways to Think Like a 21st-Century Economist*, Random House Business, 2017

[22] https://doughnuteconomics.org/tools/2 , [Derived from DEAL - doughnuteconomics.org] Creative Commons Attribution-ShareAlike 4.0 International Licence.

[23] Collier, P. and Kay, J. *Greed Is Dead: Politics After Individualism*, Penguin, 2020

[24] Tett, G. *Anthro-Vision*, Random House Business, 2021

[25] theculturetrip.com – tinyurl.com/choices288

[26] forbes.com – tinyurl.com/choices283

[27] globalcitizen.org – tinyurl.com/choices377

[28] economist.com – tinyurl.com/choices232

[29] nosaruba2025.aw – tinyurl.com/choices381

[30] nesta.org.uk – tinyurl.com/choices284

[31] citizensinformation.ie – tinyurl.com/choices289

Chapter 18 – Pulling it all Together

We began our sense-making journey by introducing four Threats that *will* disrupt our world as we move into the future. We defined a Threat as "a [person or] thing likely to cause damage or danger"[1].

There have always been threats. They will happen and when they do, the impact will be sudden and big. Threats are disruptive and it is hard to anticipate what will happen and when. They are a *potential* that disrupts people's assumptions about how things work and how people make sense of what is happening. They create watershed[2] moments, like the Covid-19 pandemic did.

Part One explored the four Threats:

- *Fractured Backbones*
- *Global Heating*
- *Breakdown of International Relations*
- *Collapse of Global Health*

You can follow the story of how each of these might emerge, and explore the Glimpses of Change to suggest ways to mitigate and adapt for their impact. We also realised – as we developed the stories – that the extent of the impact of *Global Heating, Breakdown of International Relations*, and *Collapse of Global Health*, would be very dependent on the effectiveness (or otherwise) of Backbones (see *Fractured Backbones*).

A Backbone is an agreed set of shared rules that support the way things work. Backbones can be explicit – being based upon the rule of law – or implicit – being based upon assumptions about "the way we do things around here." All Backbones are based upon agreements or assumptions that the people who rely upon them make in order to get things done effectively.

As we discussed the concept of Backbones across our network, we realised that most Backbones function on the foundation of an agreed upon Rule of Law. In today's urban, multi-cultural world, rules of law that are recognised across boundaries are fragile.

We also distinguished between mitigation and adaptation. Mitigation describes activities to avert global Threats. These activities are often dependent on public attitudes, they need to be implemented by governments in cooperation. Adaptation describes activities by which organisations or countries can recover from, or see opportunity in, or adjust to the situation after the Threat has occurred. This could be existing organisations adapting or new organisations being formed to tackle the new situation.

After exploring Threats, what could mitigate them and how organisations could adapt to their disruptions, the next stop in the sense-making journey was exploring Forces for Change. Forces for Change are qualitatively different from Threats. They are happening here and now. They are observable and often it is possible to have a good idea of which way they are going to develop. For instance, population growth is slowing down as evidenced by data on fertility rates and projections. Forces for Change will build or fade over time[3], so their progress can be tracked – and sometimes influenced. It is important to observe that these forces change direction over time. The Forces for Change are:

- *Population*
- *Urban Pull*
- *Mobility*
- *Energy Choices*
- *Connected World*
- *AI*
- *Biology*
- *Planetary Limits*
- *Economic Activity*
- *Social Change*

Each chapter has Glimpses of Change – suggesting ways that people around the world have successfully worked with each Force for Change.

Through our research on Forces for Change, we found reasons for optimism. We are, at the same time, realistic about the Threats facing the world.

We hope that our narrative has supported you to develop new ways to recognise patterns that help your sense making.

In preparation for the Possibility Wheel tool which can help you make better decisions, we'd like to share an exercise that we often do with clients. It helps you to get a visceral feel for how the different Forces for Change interact with each other and how they may impact your organisation.

This short exercise (it usually takes 45 minutes) gives you a feel for how the forces interact. It gives you and your team clear insight into the interdependence of the Forces for Change in *your* context and encourages a discussion about which is/are the most important for you and why. It is good preparation for the Possibility Wheel.

So, at the end of the day, how *do* you make robust decisions that take possible futures into account? How do you balance Forces for Change and Threats? That is what we explore in Part Three. The Possibility Wheel will help you to gain insight so that your decisions are sound, taking the appropriate Forces for Change and most important Threat into account.

> The exercise starts with an exploration of the 10 Forces for Change. Begin with a global view and then consider what it means for you and your organisation.
>
> For the exercise, note three bullet points for each Force for Change (you could use the first three bullet points from each chapter), then ask the group a question you have developed in advance, based on the three points. Create this question (about each Force for Change) so that it helps you (all) explore what it means for *your* organisation, ensuring that the question speaks to *you*. It will encourage a quick discussion so that everyone gets a feeling for each Force (and how it interacts and is interdependent with the others).
>
> Give people a minute or two to discuss (if a group is larger, break into smaller groups for the discussion). It is very quick, so just get first reactions.
>
> An example would be for Population:
> - Global reduction in population is happening faster than you think.
> - Women are having fewer children on average and there is an increasing proportion of older people.
> - Many countries in the Global North (and some in the Majority World) have a shrinking workforce supporting a growing number of older people.
>
> Your question for this example could be: "How does changing population affect our ability to hire the people we need?"
>
> When you have finished going through all the Forces for Change, ask people to decide which is the most important. They have ten minutes to discuss, decide and report back with their choice of most important Force for Change and the most surprising thing they noticed from that discussion.

---

[1] bing.com – tinyurl.com/choices234

[2] A watershed moment is a point in time when life before and life after are fundamentally different.

[3] managementtoday.co.uk – tinyurl.com/choices233

PART THREE – The Possibility Wheel

Chapter 19 – Introduction to Part Three

Threats have always been with us but we never know exactly when or how frequently they will occur. All we know is that when they do occur, it will be sudden and the impact will be big.

In Part One we introduced four of the major Threats that we are facing today: *Fractured Backbones, Global Heating, Collapse of Global Health* and *Breakdown of International Relations.*

Thinking about the potential effect of Threats is difficult for organisations. When you are planning to mitigate – or adapt to – a Threat, remember that the very definition of a Threat is that the timing is unexpected and the effects are difficult to anticipate. So, it is unlikely to happen in exactly the way you expect. As Eisenhower famously said, "Plans are worthless, but planning is everything"[1]. However, the discussion and decision process will prepare your organisation to monitor for signs that a Threat is starting to occur. This gives more time to prepare for the emerging effects and impacts.

Remember to distinguish between mitigation and adaptation in your discussion. Mitigation describes activities to avert global Threats and minimise impacts. These activities are often dependent on public attitudes, and they need to be implemented by governments and/or organisations in cooperation with their stakeholders.

Adaptation includes activities by which organisations or countries can recover from, limit impact from, or see opportunity in, the situation after a Threat has occurred. This could be existing organisations adapting themselves or new organisations being formed to tackle the new situation.

Although we have described the world in terms of Forces for Change and Threats, we know that this is a simplification. In real life, the Forces and Threats are less clear, they are interdependent, and the world itself is a complex adaptive system. As Joanna Macy explains, "Living systems evolve in complexity, flexibility, and intelligence through interaction with each other."[2] We understand that, for instance, an economic model is a simplified framework designed to illustrate complex processes. So when working with teams facing the need to make decisions, we note that the statistician George E. P. Box said, "All models are wrong, but some are useful"[3].

Knowing that the Forces for Change and the Threats are not independent, when we developed the Possibility Wheel, we identified the Forces for

Change that we thought were most likely to be affected by each Threat. The discussion to choose the group's view of these can help clarify differing opinions and assumptions. We suggest:

Threat	Forces for change most affected
Fractured Backbones	Mobility Energy Choices Connected World Economic Activity
Collapse of Global Health	Urban Pull Planetary Limits Biology Social Change
Global Heating	Energy Choices Connected World Social Change
Breakdown of International Relations	Economic Activity Planetary Limits Social Change

Making decisions is never easy. Today it seems especially problematic, with so many seismic shifts in geopolitics, climate and technology. You make better decisions when you consider different possible, plausible ways that a future may emerge and take these into account. Doing this makes your decisions more robust and resilient. You can make choices that work across several possible futures, rather than just the Business-as-Usual model that many organisations use.

In the next chapter, we introduce the Possibility Wheel and describe the Possibility Wheel Tool, step by step. It is a tool which recognises that Threats and Forces for Change affect each other. It recognises that Forces for Change and Threats have different effects in each geography and industry. It is an easy tool to use.

It will help you to quickly compare a decision taken under your current assumptions with the outcomes when your decision takes into account the Forces for Change and one important Threat. It is not a replacement for horizon scanning or futures thinking. These activities fully develop plausible stories for how a range of futures are reached and allow you to compare that range of futures. Using the Possibility Wheel provides a structured format for discussion around the possible outcomes and decisions should one particular Threat come to pass.

There are four chapters of worked examples showing how the Tool might be used. These are hypothetical examples which we have developed so that they are easy for any reader to understand. They are meant to illustrate a possible chain of logic, so bear with us even if you do not agree with the assumptions we made. They do not go into the depth that your own examples may. The examples illustrate the ways in which a decision made under current assumptions (Business-as-Usual) can be tested against a possible future where one of the Threats occurs. They have differing timescales and cover large and small private sector organisations, an NGO, and government.

Finally, we should emphasise that we have picked a set of assumptions that help illustrate the tool. The assumptions do not reflect our opinion. They are for illustration purposes only. Hopefully they will provoke discussion around your organisation's assumptions and explore the risk appetite behind decisions.

---

[1] https://quoteinvestigator.com/2017/11/18/planning/
[2] awakin.org – tinyurl.com/choices282
[3] imperial.ac.uk – tinyurl.com/choices281

Chapter 20 – The Possibility Wheel Tool

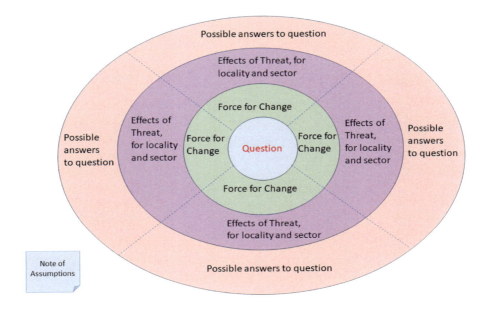

Why the Possibility Wheel?

People co-create the future through the decisions they make, so understanding the potential consequences of a decision will help to improve decision making.

The Possibility Wheel is a tool which allows you to assess the impact a Threat may have for a potential decision in a possible future. This gives insight into that decision and its consequences. The tool explores how a Threat affects the Forces for Change that are important to the question you want to make a decision about. It will help you to explore potential surprises, disruptions and backlashes as well as emerging opportunities as you face the Threat in a possible future.

The Possibility Wheel encourages a conversation about possibilities. It helps you to consider potential futures and how they could unfold. Usually, when developing futures, you will have a detailed, plausible story for how you got there. Using this tool, you are not expected to work a potential future out in great detail, although it must be plausible. Much of the value is in the discussion about different potential impacts and outcomes. It will be useful to agree your timescale for the effects in answer to your question. We encourage you to focus on a longer timescale (5-20 years) for added insight and value.

What is the Possibility Wheel?

Definition

The Possibility Wheel is a structured brainstorming tool to support decision making through organising your thinking about potential Threats, future events, issues, trends and strategy. It is a tool to encourage imagination and 'what if?' thinking: all inputs are based in an, as yet, unknown future.

What is it useful for?

- Exploring how a number of Threats may affect a decision you need to make and providing a structure to prioritise Threats so that you can work with the most important Threat for your current situation.
- Identifying and mapping connections, causalities and impacts of this specific Threat on future events, trends, issues or strategies.
- Gaining a deeper, shared understanding of how this Threat and its impacts on events and trends may play out, helping you to widen the discussion about consequences (some possibly unintended).
- Building a shared understanding of, and insights into, the impacts and consequences of this Threat on the question you want to make a decision about.

What inputs are needed?

Possibility Wheels are best developed with as diverse a team as you can manage: cross-disciplinary, cross-functional and cross-stakeholder. You will need a minimum of 6 people; you can split into breakout groups if needed. Using fewer people will yield less creativity, possibilities and opportunities.

Participants may be internal or external to the organisation but all should be aware of the organisation's strategy and its constraints.

How long do you need?

60-90 minutes for one iteration.

What Outcomes can you expect?

- A clear map of the effects of your chosen Threat on your question.
- A shared understanding of the potential consequences this Threat could have on your question, both intended and unintended.
- Notes of the assumptions you made.
- Identification of opportunities.
- Better understanding of the organisation's risk appetite.
- Insights: it is very rare that the discussion does not create some new insights – worth capturing!

The Possibility Wheel Tool

The Tool consists of seven steps.

1. Define the question you are considering (the answer will inform your decision)
2. Reach a decision based on Business-As-Usual assumptions
3. Choose the most important Threat using the weighting table
4. Fill in the Possibility Wheel for the chosen Threat over the next 5-20 years
5. Reach a decision which takes the Threat into account
6. You can repeat the last two steps, based on different assumptions
7. Compare the outcomes and evaluate the possible decisions.

The Tool will give you more robust results if you explore Possibility Wheels more than once, using different assumptions (which are likely to lead to different answers).

Step 1: Defining the question

Be clear on the question you need to answer to inform the decision that you are planning to make. Check to make sure that everyone in the team has the same understanding of what the constraints around the decision are (for example, budgets).

Step 2: Business-As-Usual Assumptions and Decision

Make the decision as you normally would in your team discussions (what we call the 'Business-As-Usual approach').

Take note of the assumptions you are making. For instance, you will be making some assumptions about how the larger environment around your organisation will act, e.g. you may consider the price of your supplies when making your decision. So write down what assumptions you are making about it and what constraints you have. You could look for an assumption around each Force for Change if that is useful. The more information you can share about what underpins your decision, the easier it will be when you come to compare it with decisions made using the Possibility Wheel.

The Note of Assumptions is an important outcome.

Step 3: Choosing the most important Threat

Threat	PEST	Implication(s) for organisation	Weight
Fractured Backbones	Political		1-3
	Economic		1-3
	Social		1-3
	Technological		1-3
		Total weight	4-12
Global Heating	Political		1-3
	Economic		1-3
	Social		1-3
	Technological		1-3
		Total weight	4-12
Breakdown of International Relations	Political		
	Economic		1-3
	Social		1-3
	Technological		1-3
		Total weight	4-12
Collapse of Global Health	Political		1-3
	Economic		1-3
	Social		1-3
	Technological		1-3
		Total weight	4-12

Threats will have different effects in different geographies and industries. The decision about the most important Threat for your organisation should be made by the group. Consider each of the four Threats and give each PEST heading a weighting between 1 and 3. Add them up to get the total weighting (between 4 and 12) for the Threat across the PEST headings. Usually you will find that one Threat will be the most disruptive for your organisation (and have the highest weighting), so work with that one.

In the worked examples you will see how these have been filled in for different cases. You can always work a second Possibility Wheel with a different Threat if that will be useful for you.

Step 4: Fill in the Possibility Wheel for the chosen Threat

Place the question you are considering in the centre of the Possibility Wheel and fill in the Wheel as follows:

a) Using the table from the *Introduction to Part Three*, place the Forces for Change that will be impacted the most by your chosen Threat in the first (green) ring of circles nearest your decision. These help you to focus by classifying the impacts you will explore. So if one of the important Forces for Change is Energy Choices, you will be exploring different impacts of Energy Choices on your business.

b) The impacts that you will be thinking about are all for a potential future (remember we suggest you think 5-20 years out), so you will have to make some assumptions. These are likely to be different to the assumptions you made for the 'Business-as-Usual' first round. These can be challenging – after all, you need to be prepared. So challenge away, it is the best way to learn. For instance, if *Global Heating* is the Threat you've identified as the most important for your organisation, what would happen if fossil fuels were outlawed? What would happen if the Greenland ice sheet started receding at thousands of feet per day?[1] Set these out so that you can refer to them later when you need to in a new Note of Assumptions. Consider what the differences are from the Business-As-Usual Assumptions.

c) The first (green) circle is for each of the Forces for Change that are impacted most by the Threat you are working with. Enter each one. You may add another Force for Change if you wish.

d) Identify the effect(s) of the Threat on each Force for Change and place in the second (purple) circle. This is where you add how your sector and geography could affect the answer to the question.

e) Explore possible answers to your initial question based on the effects for each Force for Change keeping your locality and sector in mind and place in third (peach) ring.

Here is an example of the Possibility Wheel from *Global Heating* (Chapter 22):

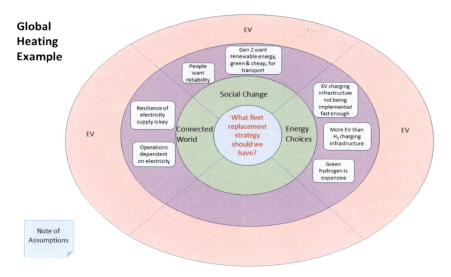

Step 5: Decision taking Threat into account

List the possible answers to your question, leading to the best decision(s) you could make for these circumstances. Using the *Example of Global Heating in Chapter 22,* (shown in the figure above), the outcome was that the Bus Fleet's replacement strategy should focus on Electric Vehicles rather than take advantage of government schemes to promote hydrogen as a fuel.

Optionally – Step 6: Repeat the last two steps with different assumptions

Repeat steps 4 and 5 using a different set of assumptions, to be able to compare how different assumptions will affect the answers and the decision(s) they have led to. The Possibility Wheel helps you to envisage different potential futures.

Step 7: Compare the outcomes and evaluate decisions

Compare the decisions you made for the Business-As-Usual discussion and the decisions resulting from using the Possibility Wheel. Having worked through the Possibility Wheel with the impact of your chosen Threat, the outcome may be different when you take the Threat into account.

If there is a difference, it may throw up new *opportunities* which can be explored. These may be for new businesses or sets of customers, or new pools of talent, or new geographies, or for merging businesses, or for new supply chains, etc.

Exploring these opportunities can help you to understand your declared vs actual *risk appetite* – you might uncover a difference. Take care not to focus too much on risks alone - your view of what is a risk will be based on your experience, not on future possibilities.

You may gain *insights* and discover that a key concern emerges which is not a factor currently on the strategic agenda. These insights could be new connections or causalities, or ideas requiring further analysis

What happens next

It is well worth exploring your learning through using the Tool.

In the next Chapters you will find the worked examples. We have picked a set of assumptions that help illustrate the tool. These are for illustration purposes only and at a high level so that they are easy to understand. They will help you explore how to use the Possibility Wheel.

Finally, the assumptions in the worked examples are illustrations and do not reflect the views of the authors!

---

[1] washingtonpost.com – tinyurl.com/choices280

Chapter 21 – Example: Fractured Backbones

Question

The Office of the Minister for Public Health needs to start contingency plans for another pandemic. The timeframe is 5-20 years and there are a number of other government departments that need to be involved. The question is: What functions are most critical to government's ability to deal with a pandemic?

The discussion in this *Example* assumes that the management team have read this book and have a working knowledge of the Forces for Change and potential Threats.

Answer under Business-as-Usual

The Minister takes soundings and is assured by the relevant departments that their contingency plans for another pandemic are in place. The relevant departments in addition to their own are Health (hospitals and doctors), Transport, Education, Treasury, Science, Immigration, Work and Pensions, and Trade.

The Minister assumes that the relevant departments will be able to supply complete, up-to-date and accurate data when requested, and provide services as defined in their contingency plans. They decide that staffing, procurement, hospital availability and the transportation network are the most important functions – so they request the departments to pay extra attention to these in their contingency plans.

Choosing the most important threat

Using the PEST table:

Threat	PEST	Implication(s) for organisation	Weight
Global Heating	Political	Rows over climate migration disrupt international agreements on public health and data sharing	1
	Economic	Climate migration puts Public Health Dept. under pressure	2
	Social	Climate migration creates areas of bad public health in overcrowded clusters	1
	Technological	Heating causes malfunction of many sensors for pollution of air and water	1
		Total weight	5
Intl Relations	Political	Wars cause massive movements of people	2
	Economic	Wars and defence spending are costly to the government and reduce funding for Public Health	2
	Social	New populations with different lifestyles affecting public health	1
	Technological	Data records hacked	1
		Total weight	6
Global Health	Political	Governments look for quick answers	2
	Economic	Budgets out of control	1
	Social	Increased inequality – those who can isolate and those who cannot	1
	Technological	Use of untried vaccines	1
		Total weight	5
Fractured Backbones	Political	Disruption of international information exchange	2
	Economic	Trade flows disrupted	2
	Social	Lack of community support, lack of respect for public sector workers	2
	Technological	Lack of connectivity as networks break down and go out of action	3
		Total weight	9

Fractured Backbones emerge as the most important threat. The table in the *Introduction to Part Three* suggests that the strongest impacts are on the following forces for change:

- Mobility
- Energy Choices

- Connected World
- Economic Activity

You may choose to add additional Forces for Change if you feel that is important for your decision.

Using the Possibility Wheel

The centre of the Possibility Wheel contains the question: 'What functions are most critical to government's ability to deal with a pandemic?'

Starting with the Forces for Change most impacted by *Fractured Backbones*, fill in the first ring of circles around the centre – Mobility, Energy Choices, Connected World and Economic Activity, as in the list above.

For the next ring, bring in local conditions. The effects of *Fractured Backbones* will depend on local geography, industry and the economy.

Mobility

- All departments will be understaffed as the public transport infrastructure shuts down.
- Private transport limited by energy shortages, affecting staff's ability to get to work and disrupting services to the public.

Energy Choices

- Energy supply will be unable to meet demand due to changes in the patterns of usage caused by working from home. This causes power failures, Cloud computing server failures and communications networks to go down.
- Hospitals will rely on back-up generators which will be old and likely to break down.

Economic Activity

- Fracture of the payments backbone means that payments cannot be made to suppliers or to employees.

Connected World

- Information exchange on the disease, on preventive measures, on vaccines, cannot happen if networks fail.

- News channels are unable to operate due to energy shortages, news is transmitted via informal channels, with distortion and perhaps causing public panics.
- Staff cannot work from home (WFH) and GPs can't consult remotely.

Assumptions and decisions

When the team analysed the threats from *Fractured Backbones*, it was clear that electricity and telecoms networks were essential to the ability of most government departments to effectively deal with the pandemic. These networks underpin mobility and economic activity. If they were fractured and not working properly, it was difficult to see how fractures in mobility or economic activity could be tackled.

So considering the potential threat from *Fractured Backbones*, the Minister for Public Health and their team realised that they should be evaluating the resilience of electricity, payments and telecoms networks and designing contingency plans based upon their resilience.

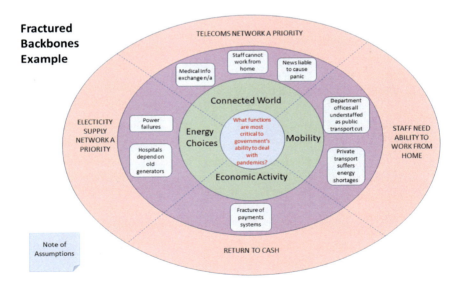

Evaluate decisions

How has the decision on the most critical functions for the government's ability to deal with a pandemic been affected by considering the threat of *Fractured Backbones*?

I. Outcomes

Under 'Business-as-Usual' the Minister's initial decision was to ask the contributing departments to pay special attention to staffing, procurement, hospital availability and transportation in their contingency plans for another pandemic.

Working through the effects of *Fractured Backbones*, the Minister realised that the key issue was the underlying backbones rather than the functions. So they asked specifically about the ability of departments to operate under *failures* of transport, energy supply, electricity, payments and telecoms network. This resulted in the establishment of a joint planning group to oversee resilience testing of transport, electricity and telecoms networks.

II. Opportunity

The availability of electricity and telecoms networks emerged as critical in managing a pandemic, since they underpin transport and payments. Therefore the opportunity is the insight which ensured that these two networks must come at the top of the resilience plan.

III. Risk Appetite

The Public Health Department initiated discussions with other Ministries to understand their exposure to *Fractured Backbones*.

IV. Insights

Public Health is dependent on information – which means electricity and telecoms networks have to come first in its resilience plans.

Chapter 22 – Example: Global Heating

Question

The manager of a fleet of buses for a regional transportation company in the UK replaces the fleet every 12 years in line with guidance. The next renewal is due in 5 years' time. The overall policy is to implement NetZero commitments. The question is: What fleet replacement strategy should we have?

The discussion in this *Example* assumes that the management team have read this book and have a working knowledge of the Forces for Change and potential Threats.

Answer under Business-As-Usual

The manager makes the decision with their team as they normally would do. They involve finance, procurement and operations.

The government has a funding scheme for hydrogen-based bus transport. The company would get government funding through regional development schemes. This seems like a good approach so they decide to take the money and go for a hydrogen fleet. The subsidies only apply to UK-manufactured hydrogen vehicles: the team check out potential suppliers and both are in early days but with ambitious plans.

Currently the most advantageous (total cost of ownership within emission limits) mix of bus fuel source is about a quarter diesel and three quarters electric[1], but the team assume that prices for hydrogen buses and infrastructure would have dropped over the next five years, and the subsidy would make up any difference. They assume that charging sources for hydrogen refuelling could be found within their network of depots and bus stations.

So under current assumptions, the choice between electricity and hydrogen as a replacement to fossil fuel for the bus fleet is hydrogen, due to government funding.

Choosing the most important Threat

Using the PEST table:

Threat	PEST	Implication(s) for organisation	Weight
Fractured Backbones	Political	Threat to supply chains	2
	Economic	Price of energy	1
	Social	Less travel	1
	Technological	Dependence on electricity	3
		Total weight	9
Global Heating	Political	International pressure away from fossil fuels	3
	Economic	High temperatures in cities, affecting mainly younger people	2
	Social	Flooding of low-lying areas	3
	Technological	Bus fleets air-conditioned	1
		Total weight	9
Intl Relations	Political	Tensions impact fossil fuel supplies	1
	Economic	Tensions impact price of fossil fuel supplies	1
	Social	Reduced public travel	1
	Technological	Faster introduction of EVs	1
		Total weight	4
Global Health	Political	Lack of international health accords	1
	Economic	Reduced incomes during pandemics	1
	Social	Reduced public travel	2
	Technological	Use of virtual connections	1
		Total weight	5

Global Heating emerges as the most important Threat. The table in the *Introduction to Part Three* chapter suggests that the strongest impacts are on the following forces for change:

- Energy Choices
- Connected World
- Social Change

You may choose to add additional Forces for Change if you feel that is important for your decision.

Using the Possibility Wheel

The centre of the Possibility Wheel contains the question: What fleet replacement strategy should we have?

Starting with the forces for change most impacted by the effects of *Global Heating*, fill in the first ring of circles around the centre – Energy Choices, Connected World, and Social Change, as in the list above.

For the next ring, bring in local conditions. The state of *Global Heating* will depend on local geography, industry and economy.

Energy Choices

- The infrastructure needed for charging vehicles is not being built as fast as is needed to service the expected increase in electric vehicles.
- But on the other hand, there are more electric charging stations being built than hydrogen charging stations.
- Green hydrogen is more expensive than grey or blue hydrogen but is better for reducing emissions than either.

Connected World

- Service to customers depends on good electricity supplies for fleet and staff management as well as powering the fleet.
- Bus fleet timetables, staff rotas and maintenance are increasingly scheduled in real time using software. This software is often supplied, maintained and operated remotely: recovery after failure is often time consuming and disruptive.

A management focus on securing electricity supplies and backup arrangements covers both needs.

Social Change

- Gen Z/Millennials care about how green their renewables are – it is currently more expensive to create green hydrogen and if it is not green hydrogen it is likely that they will not support hydrogen-powered vehicles.

- People want transportation they can count on. They will find alternatives if it is not reliable.

Assumptions and decisions

Exploring the effect of *Global Heating* locally in the UK suggests that there will be delays in decisions to invest in new technology and infrastructure. The trend towards renewables is accelerated by the Threat, but short-term thinking is pushing decisions out into the longer term.

The infrastructure for electric charging is being built much faster than for charging hydrogen-powered vehicles. Green hydrogen fuel cells are more expensive than grey or blue hydrogen fuel cells and more expensive than charging electric batteries. Younger people prefer to use public transport and prefer it to be fuelled by renewables but they do want it to be reliable.

Cheap electric buses are available as China is manufacturing for many markets. There are alternative suppliers. So electric buses (and infrastructure) are a more resilient choice.

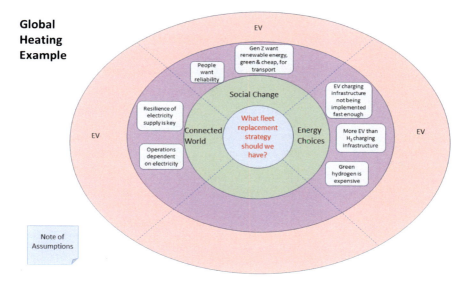

So considering the potential Threat from *Global Heating*, the choice between electricity and hydrogen bus fuel is for electricity. This is a more established vehicle technology with wider network availability and in the short term, a cheaper source of energy. The option preferred by Gen Z, creating hydrogen fuel cells from green electricity, is the most expensive charging method.

Evaluate decisions

How has the decision between electric-powered and hydrogen-powered vehicles been affected by considering the Threat from *Global Heating*?

I.   Outcomes

The initial decision was to make the choice of hydrogen-powered vehicles based on the availability of government funding and local suppliers of buses.

Working through the effects of the Threat from *Global Heating* leads to a focus on electric vehicles, as the support (maintenance, energy supply) network is more likely to be available for the older technology. It considers how the newer generations see vehicle fuelling and suggests that it is perhaps too early in the development of hydrogen charging infrastructure for it to be resilient.

II.   Opportunity

The team realised that the bus company could offer EV charging points to the community during the day when not in use by buses.

III.   Risk Appetite

Having worked their way through the Possibility Wheel, the manager and their team felt more comfortable making the decision to purchase new EV vehicles for their fleet.

IV.   Insights

For the company, as bus operators, resilience of the service emerged as their key concern.

---

[1] sciencedirect.com – tinyurl.com/choices279

Chapter 23 – Example: Breakdown in International Relations

Question

A company with operations and customers in the US and Europe needs to decide whether components should be sourced from Asia or Europe. The timeframe is 5-20 years as the company needs to maintain supplies of spares for its installed base of consumer white goods. The question is: Should we source components from Asia or Europe?

The discussion in this *Example* assumes that the management team have read this book and have a working knowledge of the Forces for Change and potential Threats

Answer under Business-as-Usual

The manager makes the decision with their team as they normally would do. They involve engineering, customer service and finance functions.

The team assumes that purchase price is key, and that in case of supply problems, a second source can be quickly found and engaged.

So under current assumptions, the choice between Asia or Europe for component suppliers is made on price alone. Asia is preferred.

Choosing the most important Threat

Using the PEST table:

Threat	PEST	Implication(s) for organisation	Weight
Fractured Backbones	Political	Threat to supply chains	2
	Economic	Price volatility	2
	Social	Reduced demand	2
	Technological	Less innovation	1
		Total weight	7
Global Heating	Political	International pressure to reduce length of supply chains to reduce emissions.	1
	Economic	High temperatures in cities, affecting mainly younger people in Asia.	1
	Social	Flooding of low-lying areas including cities and manufacturing sites in Asia.	1
	Technological	Components need better packaging to insulate in transit.	1
		Total weight	4
Breakdown of International Relations	Political	Tensions impact supply chains from Asia and potential locations of sites in Asia and Europe: water wars affect availability.	3
	Economic	Price volatility	2
	Social	Reduced demand	2
	Technological	Innovation in technology due to wars, arising from increasing international tensions.	2
		Total weight	9
Collapse of Global Health	Political	Visa restrictions for workers	1
	Economic	Reduced demand	1
	Social	Reduced demand	1
	Technological	Use of virtual connections	1
		Total weight	4

Breakdown of International Relations emerges as the most important Threat. The table in the *Introduction to Part Three* suggests that the forces for change most affected by this Threat are:
- Economic Activity
- Planetary Limits
- Social Change

You may choose to add additional Forces for Change if you feel that is important for your decision.

Using the Possibility Wheel

The centre of the Possibility Wheel contains the question: Should we source components from Asia or Europe?

The team started to collect information on sources of conflict across Asia.

Using the Forces for Change listed above, as those most impacted by the *Threat of Breakdown of International Relations*, fill in the first ring of circles around the centre – *Economic Activity, Planetary Limi*ts, and *Social Change*, as in the list above.

For the next ring, the team bring in local conditions. The effect of a *Breakdown of International Relations* will depend on local geography, industry and the economy.

Economic Activity

- SIPRI (see the Chapter on *Breakdown of International Relations*) has found that wars often arise from food insecurity, so areas with secure food supply are preferred.
- Parts of Asia that are more economically secure will be more likely to have people interested in design for sustainability: these may also be less liable to complete breakdown in case of war, allowing for timely transfers.

Planetary Limits

- Water is the crucial limit and there is no plan B: design for less water use and/or interruption of water supply but ensure that you locate plants in areas with good water supply.
- Pollution: rethink manufacturing processes to reduce waste, and locate plants of potential suppliers in areas with less air pollution as this affects people's health.

Social Change

- Gen Z and Millennials are grabbing the levers of change globally, and they are a higher proportion of the population in Asia. They buy more than older people so a concern for ethical components and production is needed. The definition of this may change by locality.

- It is difficult to anticipate which areas might be affected by a *Breakdown of International Relations*, so you will need to second/third source for production and distribution for instance, with access to multiple transport links.

Assumptions and decisions

When the team analysed their information on sources of tension across Asia and reports of potential wars and flash points, they realised the need for making continuity of supply a high priority. The prospect of 3D printing and remote servicing put emphasis on good IT connections and skills in the workforce.

When the team considered potential changes in the product line due to demographic change, they thought that being closer to markets with young people would be important. It would mean that there were more potential workers and more consumers. This would allow for tailoring of products to local conditions through requesting feedback through the supply chain and passing it to the design teams.

When the team discussed specific locations they thought that the company needed to be able to source from at least two locations, taking advantage of the diversity of cultures across Asia and spreading their risk.

The consensus was that the company should look for three sources – one in Europe and two in smaller cities in different countries in Asia.

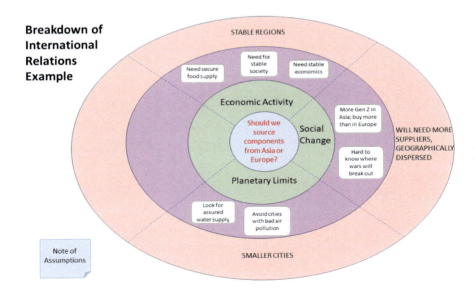

156 | The Possibility Wheel

So considering the potential from the *Breakdown of International Relations*, and the need for multiple sources of components, the choice between Asia and Europe for sourcing components is for two countries in Asia (focusing on those with young populations); and another in Europe. Choice of country(ies) will depend on assessment of potential local Breakdowns of International Relations and the skills of the local population for e.g. 3D and remote services.

Evaluate decisions

How has the decision on where to source components been affected by considering the effects of *Breakdown of International Relations*?

I. Outcomes

The initial decision was to make the choice dependent on the cost of components and assume that disruptions could be dealt with quickly by appointing a second source.

Working through the effects of *Breakdown of International Relations* leads to developing a more resilient set of sources, spread across geographies, two in Asia and one in Europe.

II. Opportunity

The team thought that once they had developed an understanding of the IT connections and skills in a few locations they could sell this knowledge to others in the network.

III. Risk Appetite

Having worked their way through the Possibility Wheel, the manager and team felt more comfortable making the decision to have several 'second' sources.

IV. Insights

For the company, its reputation depended on long lasting reliable white goods which could be supported by new technology without increasing cost.

Chapter 24 – Example: Collapse of Global Health

Question

An NGO supplying foodstuffs to the homeless and refugees, hospitals and care homes across Europe had been challenged by the shortage of wheat and cooking oil, and their price increases, due to Russia's invasion of Ukraine. They redesigned their supply chain as a result and needed to decide where other Threats could come from, so as to see how further to improve the resilience of their supply chain and delivery. The question is: How do we improve the resilience of our supply chain and delivery?

The discussion in this Example assumes that the NGO team have read this book and have a working knowledge of the Forces for Change and potential Threats.

Answer under Business-as-Usual

The manager makes decisions on the Threats that could affect the NGO with their team, as they normally do. They considered the potential for wars and civil disruption, global heating and extreme weather events on each of the major elements of the demand and the supply chain, and are content that they have taken these into account. They consider the effect of extreme weather and civil disruption on power supplies for cooking at their facilities. They make backup arrangements.

The team believe that they have taken into account all possible Threats and made plans to cover for them.

Under current assumptions, they have developed possibilities for alternative sources for foodstuffs and backup power supplies for their production facilities. They can see how to meet demand.

Choosing the most important Threat

Using the PEST table:

Threat	PEST	Implication(s) for organisation	Weight
Fractured Backbones	Political	Breakdown of supply chains due to wars.	1
	Economic	Price increases	2
	Social	Less community support	1
	Technological	Electricity breaks disrupt manufacturing capability and/or distribution by electric vehicles.	1
		Total weight	5
Global Heating	Political	Refugees from desertification add to demand	1
	Economic	Volatile prices of staples due extreme weather	1
	Social	Changes in diet due to higher temperatures in summer	1
	Technological	Power supplies hit under extreme weather conditions	2
		Total weight	5
Breakdown of Intl Relations	Political	Refugees from wars add to demand	1
	Economic	Price rises of all foodstuffs	1
	Social	Demand for different diets by people from other countries	1
	Technological	Experiments in new forms of preservation and heating for remote delivery	1
		Total weight	4
Collapse of Global Health	Political	Less international cooperation means pandemics are likely to spread globally	2
	Economic	Devastation of crops by pests or viruses could be global	3
	Social	Capacity to deliver food constrained by pandemics	2
	Technological	AMR increasing and Threats of new viruses	2
		Total weight	7

Collapse of Global Health emerges as the most important threat. The table in the *Introduction to Part Three* suggests that the strongest impacts of the *Collapse of Global Health* are on the following forces for change:

- Urban Pull
- Planetary Limits
- Biology
- Social Change

You might choose to add additional Forces for Change if you feel that is important for your decision.

Using the Possibility Wheel

The centre of the Possibility Wheel contains the question: How do we improve the resilience of our supply chain and delivery?

Starting with the forces for change most impacted by the *Collapse of Global Health*, fill in the first ring of circles around the centre with Urban Pull, Planetary Limits, Biology, and Social Change as in the list above.

For the next ring, bring in local conditions. The effect of the *Collapse of Global Health* on public health and food supplies will depend on geography, the industry and the economy.

I. *Urban pull*

- Most people live in cities – the NGO supplies the homeless, refugees, hospitals and care homes mostly in cities; so they need to understand the public health standards and policies applying in each location.
- Women have smaller families in cities – packaging small meal packs for the homeless and for refugee families as well as industrial size for hospitals and care homes.
- Pandemics spread in cities so delivery services are at risk as they are more difficult to reschedule than manufacturing shifts.

II. *Planetary Limits*

- Review water quality and improve: water is the crucial limit and there is no plan B: their production facilities rely on good quality water and one in particular is subject to contamination.
- Avoid monoculture ingredients – biodiversity is under threat – monocultures are subject to rampant diseases – which ingredients are monocultures?

III. *Biology*
- Understand the supply chain: in the same way that the green revolution has enabled the world to feed itself, work on improving crop resilience is under way but AMR (Antimicrobial Resistance) is still a threat, as are viruses such as onion viruses.
- Need to keep abreast of new technologies – regulation of new biotech lags behind implementation.

IV. *Social Change*
- Gen Z/Millennials like to know the provenance of their food and try to reduce air miles.
- Packaged meals need to be clear on food sources to ensure cultural choices e.g. halal, kosher, dairy free, etc. are met, as well as allowing for increasing dietary intolerances and allergies.

Assumptions and decisions

When the team considered *Collapse of Global Health*, they found that as well as thinking about additional potential reasons for shortages in the supply chain, they must consider the impact on their ability to reach customers in a pandemic. This led them to review the transparency of ingredients, focus on local ingredients, and explore their delivery capability as part of strategic positioning.

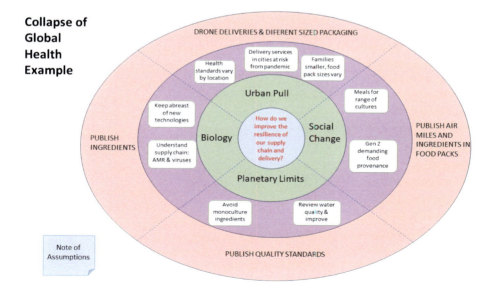

Evaluate decisions

How has the decision about the way to improve resilience of the NGO's supply change and delivery been affected by considering the *Collapse of Global Health*?

I. Outcomes

The initial decision included alternative sources for foodstuffs and backup power supplies for their production facilities.

Working through the impacts of the *Collapse of Global Health* meant that in addition to their initial thoughts, they decided to be more explicit in their listing of ingredients and airmiles; and to explore the packaging and other implications of drone deliveries to counter the loss of human delivery capacity if global health collapses.

II. Opportunity

Adoption of drone delivery could be essential in some areas during disruptions.

III. Risk Appetite

The team thought that they had already de-risked their operations and had decided that they were risk averse. Understanding additional sources of risk and following through the implications was good for their morale as they realised that they could mitigate and adapt.

IV. Insights

The team realised that there were two aspects to Threats – mitigating for the risk and adapting to it.

The earlier work on the supply chain was mitigation. Becoming more transparent, reducing air miles and implementing drone delivery was adaptation.

Chapter 25 – Insights

- Threats, disruptors and geopolitical tensions are heightening feelings of uncertainty.
- Many of the Backbones that are needed to mitigate and adapt to Threats are fractured or fracturing in today's multipolar world.
- The world faces a number of fundamental shifts in family, work, the economy, society, politics: it is a new paradigm.
- Using thinking frameworks and tools – like Threats, Forces for Change, and the Possibility Wheel tool – helps you to develop resilient choices and make more robust decisions.

You can find a summary of this book in the *Introduction*. This chapter aims to highlight our insights and allow you to refer back to the chapters which interest you.

Threats

Our first insight is that the Threats facing us are a cause of uncertainty which is more extreme than has been most people's experience in recent decades.

The common characteristics of Threats are that changes in the status quo are likely to be sudden, with outcomes that are difficult to imagine and plan for. When a Threat occurs, it disrupts the Forces for Change and any decisions that you might wish to make. The Threats of *Global Heating*, *Breakdown in Internal Relations* and *Collapse of Global Health* are already disrupting – or have recently disrupted - people's lives across the world as we write.

Global Heating is about the climate and ecological change that the world faces. It is already a big disruptor in many parts of the planet. There are many facets to this Threat, the biggest being the uncertainty the world faces around when the changes become irreversible; what exactly the changes will be; and what (and where) their impacts will be. The WEF's top four global risks over ten years are all climate change related[1]: extreme weather events; critical changes in Earth systems; biodiversity loss and ecosystem collapse; natural resource shortages. Pollution is also in the top ten.

In *Breakdown of International Relations* we explore how nations behave with one another, including trade and/or war. Many factors contribute to underlying shifts in global order and power. While the shifts may be gradual, there are often a number of indicator events that precede disruptive change.

For much of the last century the USA was the leading power in setting the world order – this is unlikely to remain true for the rest of this century. At the time of writing it seems likely that China will continue to expand its global footprint and that some middle ranked (by GDP) countries will endure wars. Economic power is becoming more diffuse; an array of powers will likely seek to assert their presence on the global stage in a multipolar world.

In the world today, illness, pandemics and disease are disruptors and a Threat to society as well as to individuals – we consider this under the broader heading of *Collapse of Global Health*. There have always been incurable, fatal infectious diseases which have disrupted societies. What is certain is that there will be another global health crisis, though we do not yet know its cause, when it will strike, or its characteristics[2].

The Threats are explored individually as if they are independent of each other. This is a simplification which makes it easier to explain what they are and what is happening – and could happen – in the future. They are of course inter-related; for instance, *Global Heating* could cause the *Collapse of Global Health* in a disaster; *Breakdown of International Relations* constrains the communication channels for discussing and agreeing measures to mitigate *Global Heating*.

After searching for the thread that linked the three (widely recognised) Threats, we did, indeed find one. We defined it as a new metaphor which we call *Fractured Backbones*.

Fractured Backbones

A second useful insight is that the health (or otherwise) of Backbones is an important factor in mitigating or adapting to the impact of the other three Threats.

Fractured Backbones looks at how the rules of the game are (or are not) working. As we discussed this concept across our network, we realised that Backbones can only function when based on the foundation of an accepted Rule of Law and a set of agreed assumptions about the way things work.

Societies design Backbones – sets of rules and assumptions – to enable people to get things done. Effective Backbones allow people to work, communicate, and solve problems together successfully. When Backbones work well, they provide the resilience needed to adapt to other Threats.

A number of Backbones which have been important over past decades are no longer fit for purpose and are fractured or fracturing, rather than evolving.

In this century, one of society's challenges is to maintain these Backbones or to replace them with others in a way that allows societies with different cultures to adapt and continue to work together.

It is not all bad news about Backbones. For instance, NATO is an example of a Backbone that has been modified and strengthened to meet a crisis – the invasion of Ukraine by Russia. This may provide a template for other international organisations as they face the need to evolve. And when people were faced with the Covid-19 pandemic, collaboration between scientists across the world (a Backbone) helped to develop effective vaccines in record time. Understanding this metaphor can be a step towards strengthening and evolving Backbones.

Fundamental shifts

Our third insight is that society is facing a number of fundamental shifts towards a new paradigm which include shifts in family, work, the economy and politics. These shifts are due to trends which are observable – Forces for Change which are discussed in *Part Two*.

It is often possible to have a good idea of which way these are developing. For instance, many countries will continue to grapple with an ageing population, combining a long-term rise in life expectancy with declining fertility rates. In contrast, Africa faces a different policy challenge: by 2030, young Africans are expected to constitute nearly half of global youth (see *Population*). A major shift over the past decades has been due to the trend from a predominantly rural world to one in which most people live in towns and cities, as we describe in *Urban Pull*. *Urban Pull* changes lifestyles through improved education, healthcare and employment opportunities. One societal result of *Urban Pull* is that people from many different cultures now live together in cities. That this is mostly amicable is a positive statement about humankind.

The move out of poverty has been based on the use of energy – to date mostly fossil fuels (described in *Energy Choices*) and for travel and transport (explored in *Mobility*). The energy used in transport is changing from fossil fuels, while travel for leisure is rebounding after the Covid-19 pandemic.

The world has become a *Connected World* based on computers, a multiplicity of devices and networks. The positive and negative social and economic implications of this are far reaching. Technology is a major factor in the new paradigm, as it can be used to create virtual worlds, exempt from physical limits. In the next decade, the technologies described in *Connected World*, *AI* (Artificial Intelligence) and *Biology* could allow the world to reduce its dependence on fossil fuels, the pollution from travel and transport, and tackle the physical constraints we described in *Planetary Limits*. As optimists, we see a precedent in the Green Revolution, which revolutionised food supplies worldwide. Advances in *Biology* are now revolutionising human, animal and plant health at an amazing rate.

AI and robots outperform humans in a range of applications (but by no means all), while the weaknesses are becoming apparent – algorithms reinforce existing biases, and false results are not easily checked. As we write, governments are discussing how to regulate the application of AI effectively. Other key technologies expected to develop rapidly over the next ten years include quantum computing and brain-computer interfaces, all bringing risks and benefits with unknown effects.

Economic Activity tells the story of how the world – particularly Asia – has seen people's incomes increasing. When people have enough money to make more life choices, quality of life becomes more important. They choose to move to cities to improve their lives. The downside is that many cities in the Majority World have polluted air and poor water quality[3].

Meanwhile, the increased role of IT-enabled platforms is changing the skills needed in many industries and developing a gap between high and low earners, leading to rising inequality. It is increasing the potential for remote working, particularly tapping into skills in countries with educated people. The global economy today is very different from that in the last century, with disruptive social effects. In the Global North, fertility rates are declining and inward migration is increasing. In the Majority World, differences are visible between economies with a growing middle class and those with industries which do not encourage this.

One result of the Covid-19 pandemic was to provide a role model for international cooperation to tackle big problems, in the amazing feat of developing vaccines at pace. Another has been to accelerate a rethinking of value systems and the nature of work and the family, with new social structures emerging to replace those that are fragmenting. We remarked earlier on the effect of *Urban Pull*. Politics and leadership, both national and international, are already changing. We explore this in *Social Change*.

Part Two has a chapter describing each of the ten Forces for Change as if they were independent of each other. This is of course a simplification, but it does allow you to start an informed dialogue. In real life, the Forces and Threats are less clear cut and separate. Rather they are interdependent, and the world itself is a complex adaptive system. As Joanna Macy explains, "Living systems evolve in complexity, flexibility, and intelligence through interaction with each other."[4]

Some of the interconnections are identified in the chapters on *Economic Activity* and *Social Change*, where we refer back to the Forces for Change which have contributed and are contributing to the new paradigm.

One aspect of the new paradigm is that, more than ever before in history, people can make their own choices, with many freed from poverty and empowered by education and a connected world. This means that people are enabled to use their human traits of communication and collaboration, as Rutger Bregman highlights in *Humankind*[5].

What does it mean to be a human being as the world changes? Being human in a potential future does, of course, require many of the same skills we use today. In addition, the massively changed context and options demand that people develop new ways of cooperating across cultures, outside the family or tribe. What being human means is changing as societies and economies around the world change.

Resilient Choices and Decision making – the Possibility Wheel

The final insight was that combining evidence from real-world data with thinking frameworks and tools – like Threats, Forces for Change, and the Possibility Wheel – allows you to develop resilient choices and make more robust decisions.

The Possibility Wheel is a tool which allows you to assess how a decision is affected by a potential Threat. It gives insight into the decision and its consequences by exploring how the Threat affects the Forces for Change that are important to the decision. It will help you to investigate surprises, disruptions and backlashes as well as emerging opportunities, from which to develop resilient choices.

To help decision makers, when we developed the Possibility Wheel, we identified the Forces for Change which we thought were most likely to be affected by each Threat. You will find a table in *The Possibility Wheel Tool* which lists these. The discussion to choose the group's view of which Threat is most important can help clarify differing opinions and assumptions.

The *Possibility Wheel Tool* describes the process in seven steps.

1. Define the question you need to answer before making your decision.
2. Reach a decision based on Business-As-Usual assumptions.
3. Choose the most important Threat based on a PEST analysis.
4. Fill in the Possibility Wheel for the Threat thinking medium to long-term.
5. Reach a possible decision which takes the Threat into account.
6. You can repeat the last two steps, based on different assumptions.
7. Compare the outcomes and evaluate the possible decisions.

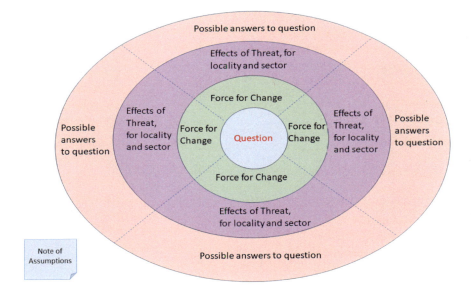

The process will give you more resilient choices if you use the Possibility Wheel more than once, with different assumptions.

We include four chapters of worked examples, each considering one of the four potential Threats as it impacts a decision. The worked examples are for the purpose of illustration and the assumptions incorporated are not necessarily those of the authors!

Finally

Threats, disruptors and geopolitical tensions are unparalleled in recent times, heightening feelings of uncertainty. The world faces a number of fundamental shifts in family, work, the economy, society, politics: it is a new paradigm. Backbones that are needed to mitigate and adapt to Threats are fractured or fracturing in today's multipolar world.

Using thinking frameworks and tools – like Threats, Forces for Change, and the Possibility Wheel tool – helps you to develop resilient choices and make better, more robust decisions.

This book helps you to take a step back from the day-to-day to get a bigger picture and enables you to explore potential futures through evidence of what is happening in the world today.

Making sense of the data describing the external world and feeding that into the Possibility Wheel Tool will lead to more resilient choices and robust decisions. We hope that this book gives you the confidence to improve your decision making.

What other challenges are people facing today? What kind of a world would people like to create? The tools and data exist for people to collaborate. People are wanting change. Putting people, data and tools together is *the* opportunity for the next decades. Over to you.

---

[1] samiconsulting.co.uk – tinyurl.com/choices376

[2] Gilbert, S. and C. Green, *Vaxxers, a pioneering moment in scientific history.* Hodder & Stoughton, 2022

[3] sciencedirect.com – tinyurl.com/choices375

[4] awakin.org – tinyurl.com/choices374

[5] Bregman, R., *Humankind, a Hopeful History*, Bloomsbury Publishing, 2020

Appendix 1 – UN Sustainable Development Goals for 2030

The Sustainable Development Goals (SDGs) are a collection of 17 interlinked global goals designed to be a "blueprint to achieve a better and more sustainable future for all". The SDGs were set up in 2015 by the United Nations General Assembly and are intended to be achieved by the year 2030.

Each of these goals has a number of targets, a total of 169 in all.

Goal 1: End poverty in all its forms everywhere.

Goal 2: End hunger, achieve food security and improved nutrition and promote sustainable agriculture.

Goal 3: Ensure healthy lives and promote wellbeing for all, at all ages.

Goal 4: Ensure inclusive and equitable quality education and promote lifelong learning opportunities for all.

Goal 5: Achieve gender equality and empower all women and girls.

Goal 6: Ensure availability and sustainable management of water and sanitation for all.

Goal 7: Ensure access to affordable, reliable, sustainable and modern energy for all.

Goal 8: Promote sustained, inclusive and sustainable economic growth, full and productive employment and decent work for all.

Goal 9: Build resilient infrastructure, promote inclusive and sustainable industrialisation and foster innovation.

Goal 10: Reduce inequality within and among countries.

Goal 11: Make cities and human settlements inclusive, safe, resilient and sustainable.

Goal 12: Ensure sustainable consumption and production patterns.

Goal 13: Take urgent action to combat climate change and its impacts.

Goal 14: Conserve and sustainably use the oceans, seas and marine resources for sustainable development.

Goal 15: Protect, restore and promote sustainable use of the terrestrial ecosystems, sustainably manage forests, combat desertification, and halt and reverse land degradation and halt biodiversity loss.

Goal 16: Promote peaceful and inclusive societies for sustainable development, provide justice for all and build effective, accountable and inclusive institutions at all levels.

Goal 17: Strengthen the means of implementation and revitalise the Global Partnership for Sustainable Development.

Appendix 2 – Terminology and some sources of data

People have differing capabilities and circumstances. We have introduced terminology to describe 'people' in more detail – their generation and their living standard.

We distinguish generations with different characteristics: these are Traditionalists or The Silent Generation (born before 1945), Baby Boomers (born between 1945 and 1965), Generation X (born between 1965 and 1980), Millennials – also known as Generation Y – (born between 1980 and 2000) and Generation Z (born after 2000)[1].

We use an economic scale defined by the UN to describe people's living standard. This scale uses a simplified labelling system: Levels 1, 2, 3 and 4. Levels 3 and 4 are often defined as 'middle class'. Middle class for us is a positive phrase because it means that people have enough income to be able to exercise choice.

A quick aide memoire, based on that used by Hans Rosling in his book *Factfulness*[2], for each Level is (with approximate numbers as of 2019):

Level	Billions	Access to water
1	1	Your five children take turns to walk barefoot to a hole an hour's walk away with your only bucket.
2	3	It only takes half an hour to fetch fresh water for the day as you have a bicycle and several buckets.
3	2	You have your own cold water tap and access to electricity or gas to heat the water up.
4	1	You have hot and cold water on tap indoors.

We have used many sources of historical data and also some for predictions. Below are the ones we used most frequently. Other more specialised sources are referenced in the text where relevant.

- The World Bank is a rich source of data on a range of topics from implementation of the UN SDGs to urban development to the number of people in poverty.

https://data.worldbank.org

- The United Nations provides data on a wide range of topics including population projections and on migration/refugees.
  http://data.un.org

- The International Energy Agency covers both energy and CO_2 emissions by energy type, including renewables.
  https://www.iea.org

- The commercial data firm Statista provides paid-for market reports and many free infographics based on their data.
  https://www.statista.com

- BP provides extensive analysis and projections for energy demand and supply.
  https://www.bp.com/en/global/corporate/energy-economics/energy-outlook.html

- Our World in Data is about research and data to make progress against the world's largest problems. Visualisations and text are under the Creative Commons BY license. You may freely use these for any purpose and data is available for download.
  https://ourworldindata.org/

---

[1] theconversation.com – tinyurl.com/choices373

[2] Rosling, H., Rosling, O., et. al. *Factfulness: Ten Reasons We're Wrong About the World - And Why Things Are Better Than You Think*. Sceptre. 2019

Index

adaptation, 13, 36, 44, 127, 133, 162; difference from mitigation, 4, 10; to impacts, 20
ageing, 12, 41, 56, 117, 165; in China, 88; and neural interfaces, 97
Amazon, the, 102
American Economic Liberties Project, 114
Antarctica, 24
antibiotics, 41-43, 88
antimicrobials, 41
Arévalo, Bernardo, 22
Aruba, 125
Asian Development Bank, 17
ASIMO, 92
Association of Professional Futurists, ix, 44, 179
Attenborough, Sir David, 58
autonomous vehicles, 67-69

Bangladesh, 112
batteries, 76, 77, 151
Bekele, Heman, 123
Berlin, 63
biodiversity, 100-104, 111, 125, 160, 163, 171
Birol, Fatih, 2
Black, Maggie, 103
blockchain, 21, 81, 109
Boneva, Teodora, 29
Boot, Max, 36, 37, 39
Box, G. P., 49, 133
Bregman, Rutger, 3, 6, 167, 169
Bremmer, Ian, 11, 14

Brodin, Jasper, 3
Buffet, Warren, 58
Bullough, Oliver, 110, 115, 119
Buontempo, Carlo, 26
California, 101
Carbfix, 28
Carbon Footprint think tank, 74
Cereol, 98
Chandrayaan-3, 69
ChatGPT, 89-91
China, 11-12, 15-18, 30-34, 55, 57, 74, 76, 81, 87-90, 93, 102-105, 108, 118, 121, 151, 164; Belt and Road Initiative, 21, 34, 67; electricity generation, 77; floods, 26; maglev, 67; robot use, 88; solar power, 28; vehicle market, 70
cities, 50, 54, 60-68, 85, 86, 100, 107, 109, 118, 149, 154, 156, 160, 165-166, 170; 15-minute cities, 64; coastal, 25, 29; design of, 65; Smart, 62, 68, 81-2; *See also* urban pull
Citizens' Assembly, 125
climate change, 2, 13, 18, 20, 27, 35, 41, 64, 111, 119, 123, 125, 163, 170; and CO_2 emitters, 28; Copernicus Climate Change Service, 26; and desertification, 24, 29, 159; and El Niño, 26, 30; and sea levels, 24-25, 29-30; and sorghum, 29; and Aerosol Injection, 28-29
CO_2 emissions, 73, 74, 173
Colony Collapse Disease, 101

commander's intent, 37
Covid-19, 1, 9, 13, 18, 21, 27, 37, 40-44, 51, 82, 85, 96, 109, 113, 123, 127, 165, 166; and cash use, 81; and cities, 61; and cycling, 67; and disease spread, 56; and inequality, 118; and travel, 71; and vaccines, 100
CRISPR, 95-98
cryptocurrency, 81, 124
CyArk, 71
cyborgs, 97

Davos World Economic Forum, 1
De Hogeweyk, 58
democracy, 13, 22-23, 32, 83, 111, 115, 119-126
Democracy Index, 120
Doughnut Economics, 111, 115, 122, 126
drones, 32, 36, 80, 87-88, 91, 92
Duchenne muscular dystrophy, 98

enzyme replacement therapy, 96

Federal Trade Commission, 84, 114
food shortages, 100
Forces for Change
    AI, v, 11, 12, 50, 52, 70, 72, 82, 87-93, 109, 118-119, 128, 166
    Biology, v, 11, 50, 52, 94-99, 100, 103, 117, 119, 128, 134, 160, 161, 166
    Connected World, v, 50, 52, 68, 80-86, 100, 109, 113, 118, 123-124, 128, 134, 145, 149-150, 166
    Economic Activity, v, 18, 38, 50, 51, 55, 80, 107-116, 119, 124, 128, 134, 145, 154-155, 166, 167
    Energy Choices, v, 49-51, 73-79, 128, 134, 140, 144-145, 149-150, 165
    Mobility, v, 50-51, 62, 63, 66-72, 119, 128, 134, 144-145, 165
    Planetary Limits, v, 50, 51, 96, 100-107, 111, 119, 128, 134, 154-155, 160, 166
    Population, vii, 4, 15-18, 29, 40, 41, 49, 53-63, 75, 80, 88, 101, 103, 104, 107, 109, 117, 125, 128, 155-157, 165, 173 +6+.0-
    Social Change, v, 12, 51, 52, 80, 110, 111, 117-126, 128, 134, 149, 150, 154-155, 160-161, 166, 167
    Urban Pull, v, 50-54, 60-65, 100, 107, 118, 128, 134, 160, 165, 166
Friedman, Thomas, 34
Future of Skills, 89

Gates, Bill, 28, 30
gene editing, 94-97
Generation Z, 118, 119, 172
genetic modification, 94
Genome Editing, 95
global heating, 24, 26-29, 73, 95, 158
Golden Arches Theory, 34
Goodall, Jane, 58
Google, 71, 111, 114
green revolution, 6, 94, 161
Himalayas, 24
Houghton, John, 24, 30, 93
hydro-electricity, 75

hydrogen, 28, 67-70, 76, 78, 141, 148, 150-152

iFlytek, 92
IMF, 17, 18, 83
infant mortality, 43
International Criminal Court, 20, 37
International Energy Agency, 67, 75, 173

Jakarta, 30
Japan, vii, 55-56, 74, 88, 90, 92, 104, 120

Kanter, Jonathan, 114
Kerala, 54
Kolbert, Elizabeth, 101, 105, 106

London Underground, 71

MacAskill, William, 4, 6, 11-14, 27, 30
Magh Mela, 92
malaria, 13, 43, 51
McRae, Hamish, 12, 14, 51-52, 120, 125
Meadows, Donella, 59, 100
Mercedes-Benz Trucks, 70
mitigation, 4, 10, 13, 91, 127, 133, 162
M-KOPA, 77
Montreal Protocol, 19, 35
M-Pesa, 84, 86, 113, 124

NASA, 30
National Health Service, 16
National Highway Traffic Safety Administration, 69
National Security Risk Assessment, 13, 20
National Thermal Power Corporation, 78
NATO, 17, 19, 33, 165
Nepal, 85, 124
Netherlands, 58, 98, 103
North Pacific Gyre, 100
nuclear power, 74, 76, 79

Obama, Barack, 120, 125
OECD, 67, 77, 109, 114
Omand, Sir David, 10, 14, 23

pandemics, 11-13, 40, 41, 50, 111, 149, 159, 164
Pew Research Center, 83
Pinker, Steven, 32, 38
platforms, 17, 18, 34, 50, 80-81, 84, 90, 109, 117, 166
pollution, 40, 50, 61, 66, 74, 90, 96, 99, 100, 144, 155, 166
Population, v, 12, 33, 38, 49-55, 57, 61, 62, 114, 117, 123, 128, 165
Porras, Consuelo, 22
pragmatic optimists, 2, 3, 13
Putin, Vladimir, 20, 22, 37, 38

Quaas, Johanna, 58

Raworth, Kate, 111, 115, 122, 126
Ritchie, Hannah, 2, 6, 23, 30
rivers, 24, 64, 102, 103
robots, 50, 87, 88, 92, 109, 166
Rockstrom, Johan, 101
Roubini, Nouriel, 12, 14

Royal Mint, 113
Royal Netherlands Institute for Sea Research, 98
rule of law, 4, 15, 22, 38, 121, 127

Sardar, Ziauddin, 121
Science and Technology Agreement, 18
SDGs, 5, 19, 170, 172
second movers, 37
Serreze, Mark, 24
Singapore, 70, 83, 120
Slum Networking project, 64
smart cities, 68, 82, 86
solar power, 28, 75
South Korea, 55, 76, 88, 90, 113
space, 30, 32, 42, 62, 64, 70, 72, 81, 102, 104, 109; junk, 20; tourism, 69
Stockholm International Peace Research Institute, 32, 35
Stoller, Matt, 114
Suez Canal, blocked, 18
Superintelligence, 87
telecoms networks, 146, 147
Tett, Gillian, 1, 6, 115, 123, 126
Threats
    Breakdown of International Relations, v, 11-13, 18, 32, 34, 36, 104, 112, 123, 127, 133-134, 139, 154-157, 164
    Collapse of Global Health, v, 9, 11-13, 18, 40, 42, 44, 63, 97, 104, 123, 127, 133-134, 139, 154, 158-164
    Fractured Backbones, v, 1, 4, 9-15, 17, 19, 20, 33, 35, 41-42, 69, 77, 91, 111-112, 127, 133, 134, 139, 143-149, 154, 159, 164
    Global Heating, v, 4, 9-13, 18, 24, 27-30, 33, 34, 51, 77, 84, 102, 103, 123, 127, 133-134, 139-144, 148,-154, 159, 163, 164
Transform Freetown, 63
Tsinghua University, 92

Ubuntu, 123
Ukraine: Russian invasion, 17, 33, 36, 38, 73, 88, 124, 158, 165
UN: Food & Agriculture Organisation, 19; Security Council, 10, 17, 33; Sustainable Development Goals, v, 5, 170
UNICITI, 63

Volvo Construction Equipment, 28

Watts, Laura, 78, 79
weapons of mass destruction, 33
wind power, 76, 78
Women Waging Peace Network, 35
World Bank, 17, 18, 107, 111-115, 172
World Economic Forum, 82, 83, 110
World Food Program, 35
World Health Organization, 41, 43, 56
World Trade Organisation, 17

Zander, Benjamin, 58
Zhanglu, Tan, 82, 86
Zoom, 44, 85

About the Authors

Patricia Lustig is an internationally recognised practitioner in foresight and strategy development, future thinking, scenario planning and innovation. She has worked globally and is multilingual.

Patricia is a Board Member of the Association of Professional Futurists (APF) and Programme Director of their flagship Emerging Fellows Programme. She runs LASA Insight Ltd. and works with SAMI Consulting.

She wrote the award winning *Strategic Foresight: Learning from the future*, has written 6 further books and publishes blogs and articles through Long Finance, APF, Radix often with Gill Ringland and on her Substack, *It's Not All Bad*.

She can be contacted via patricia@lasa-insight.com

Gill Ringland is an Emeritus Fellow of SAMI Consulting.

She is a Life Fellow of the BCS. She is an ICL Fellow Emeritus and a Fellow of the World Academy of Art & Science.

She wrote *Scenario Planning* while responsible for strategy at ICL. She has over 150 publications and her books are used at Business Schools including Harvard. This is her twelfth book She publishes thought pieces and blogs through the BCS, Long Finance, the apf and Radix, often with Patricia Lustig.

She can be contacted via gillringland@gmail.com

About the Publisher

Triarchy Press is an independent publisher of alternative thinking about possible futures for government, organisations and society at large – as well as the creative lives of the people who participate in them.

Other related titles include:

Dancing at the Edge: Competence, Culture and Organization in the 21st Century (Maureen O'Hara and Graham Leicester)

Designing Regenerative Cultures (Daniel Christian Wahl)

Growing Wings on the Way: Systems Thinking for Messy Situations (Rosalind Armson)

Humanising Healthcare: Patterns of Hope for a System Under Strain (Margaret Hannah)

Imagining After Capitalism (Andy Hines)

Managing the Future: A Guide to Forecasting and Strategic Planning in the 21st Century (Stephen M. Millett)

Ready for Anything: Designing Resilience for a Transforming World (Tony Hodgson)

Strategic Foresight: Learning from the Future (Patricia Lustig)

The Decision Loom: A Design for Interactive Decision-Making in Organizations (Vince Barabba)

Three Horizons: The Patterning of Hope (Bill Sharpe)

Thrivability: Breaking Through to a World that Works (Jean Russell)

Transformative Innovation: A Guide to Practice and Policy for System Transition (Graham Leicester)

For details of all these titles, visit
www.triarchypress.net/possiblefutures